INDIAN COUNCIL OF HISTORICAL RESEARCH
MONOGRAPH SERIES

INDIAN EMIGRANTS TO
SUGAR COLONIES

INDIAN EMIGRANTS TO SUGAR COLONIES

A Study through Calcutta Port 1842–1900

SUTAPA DAS DHAR

CHANDRALEKHA BASU GHOSH

IHR

INDIAN COUNCIL OF HISTORICAL RESEARCH

in association with

PRIMUS BOOKS

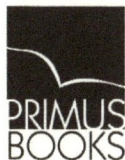

PRIMUS BOOKS

An imprint of Ratna Sagar P. Ltd.
Virat Bhavan
Mukherjee Nagar Commercial Complex
Delhi 110 009

Offices at

CHENNAI LUCKNOW

AGRA AHMEDABAD BANGALORE COIMBATORE
DEHRADUN GUWAHATI HYDERABAD JAIPUR JALANDHAR
KANPUR KOCHI KOLKATA MADURAI MUMBAI
PATNA RANCHI VARANASI

First published 2017

ISBN: 978-93-84082-88-8 (hardback)
ISBN: 978-93-84092-96-2 (POD)
ISBN: 978-93-84092-97-9 (e-book)

Published by Primus Books

in association with

INDIAN COUNCIL OF HISTORICAL RESEARCH
35 Ferozeshah Road, New Delhi 110001

Laser typeset by Guru Typograph Technology
Crossings Republic, Ghaziabad 201 009

Printed and bound in India by Replika Press Pvt. Ltd.

Our revered research advisor

PROFESSOR DURGAPRASAD BHATTACHARYYA

Contents

List of Tables and Appendices   ix

Preface   xiii

Acknowledgements   xvii

PART I

1. Colonial Emigration   3
2. Sugar Colonies: Economic Conditions and Rules
   Relating to Emigration   13

PART II

3. Extent of Emigration: Causes and Decline   31
4. Effects of Emigration   53
5. Conclusion   77

   Appendices   82

   Bibliography   113

   Index   119

Tables and Appendices

TABLES

1.1   Number of Emigrants to Mauritius from Calcutta, Madras, Bombay, 1843   6

1.2   The Colonies and the Number of Indian Population, 1882   7

2.1   Statement showing Sugar Exports from Mauritius during the Period 1846–52   15

2.2   The Terms Offered to Intending Emigrants to the Four Sugar Colonies under British Possession since 1871   25–7

3.1   Statement Showing Number of Emigrants to Mauritius, Demerara, Trinidad and Jamaica through Calcutta Port from Some Selected Provinces during 1872–3   35

3.2   District-wise Distribution of Emigrants to Mauritius during the Year 1851 and 1854–5   36

3.3   Proportion of Emigrants from Bihar, NWP and Oudh to Four Sugar Colonies during 1875–6 to 1899–1900   37

3.4   Statement showing Number of Emigrants to Demerara, Trinidad, Jamaica and Mauritius from Some Selected Districts of Bengal, Bihar, NWP and Oudh through Calcutta Port during 1870–1 and 1893   38

3.5   Places of Birth of a Sample of Emigrants from India to British Guiana, 1865–1917   39

3.6   Proportion of Emigrants within the Age Group 20–30 years to the Four Sugar Colonies during 1875–6 to 1899–1900   39

3.7   Age and Sex of Immigrants from India to British Guiana during the period 1865–1917   40

3.8   Religion and Caste of a Sample of Emigrant from Calcutta to British Guiana, 1865–1917   41

3.9   Percentage of Migrant Workers in Certain Mills, Factories and Industrial Concerns in 24 Parganas, Howrah, and Hooghly Districts of Bengal, 1897   44

3.10   Immigrants to the Industrial Districts of Bengal from Outside Bengal, 1891   45

3.11   Immigrants to the Industrial Districts of Bengal from Outside Bengal, 1901   45

4.1   Size of Plots Purchased by Indian Immigrants, 1850–9 to 1880–4   56

4.2   Home Districts of Indian Immigrants Purchasing Portion of 'Belle Mare' Estate and the Terrain Currie, 1879–84   56

4.3   Annual Savings of Mauritian and Indian Agricultural Class in the Government Savings Banks of Mauritius, 1851, 1855   58

4.4   Statement Showing the Number of Emigrants through Calcutta Port who Proceeded to and Returned from Four Sugar Colonies for the Decades 1842–50, 1851–60, 1861–70, 1871–80, 1881–90 and 1891–8   62

4.5   Percentage of Mortality on the Voyage from Calcutta to Mauritius, Demerara, Trinidad and Jamaica during 1859–70   66

4.6   Percentage of Mortality in the Vessel among the Emigrants Carried to the Sugar Colonies during 1883–84 to 1889–90   66

APPENDICES

I   Gross Emigration from British India to Four Sugar Colonies and through Calcutta Port, 1842–1900   82–5

II-A   Annual Return of Emigrants by Age Despatched to Mauritius through Calcutta Port during the Period 1875–6 to 1899–1900   86

II-B   Annual Return of emigrants by age despatched to Demerara through Calcutta Port during the Period 1875–6 to 1899–1900   87

II-C   Annual Return of Emigrants by Age Despatched to
         Trinidad through Calcutta Port during the Period
         1875–6 to 1899–1900   88

II-D   Annual Return of Emigrants by Age Despatched to
         Jamaica through Calcutta Port during the Period
         1875–6 to 1899–1900   89

III-A   Statement Showing Sex Ratio of Emigrants Despatched
         through Calcutta Port to Four Sugar Colonies during
         1842–70   90

III-B   Statement Showing Sex Ratio of Emigrants Despatched
         through Calcutta Port to Four Sugar Colonies during
         1877–8 to 1899–1900   91

IV-A   Annual Return of Emigrants Despatched through
         Calcutta Port Distributed by Caste and Religion for
         the Years 1877–8 to 1899–1900   92

IV-B   Annual Return of Emigrants Despatched through
         Calcutta Port Distributed by Caste and Religion
         for the Years 1877–8 to 1899–1900   93

IV-C   Annual Return of Emigrants Despatched through
         Calcutta Port Distributed by Caste and Religion
         for the Years 1877–8 to 1899–1900   94

IV-D   Annual Return of Emigrants Despatched through
         Calcutta Port Distributed by Caste and Religion
         for the Years 1877–8 to 1899–1900   95

V-A   Places whence Emigrants Came to Calcutta for
         Embarkation to Mauritius during the Period 1874–5
         to 1899–1900   96

V-B   Places whence Emigrants came to Calcutta for
         Embarkation to Demerara during the period 1874–5
         to 1899–1900   97

V-C   Places whence Emigrants came to Calcutta for
         Embarkation to Trinidad during the Period 1874–5
         to 1899–1900   98

V-D   Places whence Emigrants came to Calcutta for
         Embarkation to Jamaica during the Period 1874–5
         to 1899–1900   99

VI   Statement Showing the Number of East Indian
          Emigrants who have Returned Calcutta from the
          Four Sugar Colonies with the Amount of their
          Savings, Remittances, etc., during the Period 1872–3
          to 1899–1900   100–1

VII-A   Statement Showing the Number of Emigrants
          Previously Returned from Mauritius and
          Re–emigrated to the Various Colonies during the
          Period 1877–8 to 1889–90 and 1893–4   102

VII-B   Statement Showing the Number of Emigrants
          Previously Returned from Demerara and
          Re–emigrated to the Various Colonies during the
          Period 1877–8 to 1889–90 and 1893–4   103

VII-C   Statement Showing the Number of Emigrants
          Previously Returned from Trinidad and Re–emigrated
          to the Various Colonies during the Period 1877–8
          to 1889–90 and 1893–4   104

VII-D   Statement Showing the Number of Emigrants
          Previously Returned from Jamaica and Re–emigrated
          to the various colonies during the period 1877–7 to
          1889–90 and 1893–4   105

VIII   Statement of Mortality in Depots among
          Emigrants and Causes of Deaths during 1877–78
          to 1889–90   106–8

IX   Statement Showing the Commencement and
          Resumption of Emigration to Four Sugar Colonies,
          in Regular System from India, 1842–1900   109–10

X   Proportion of Brahmin/Higher Caste to Total
          Emigrants from Calcutta Port to Four Sugar
          Colonies, Mauritius, Demerara, Trinidad and Jamaica
          during 1877–8 to 1898–9   111

Preface

INDIAN EMIGRATION TO plantation colonies has been a subject of intense historical interest for many years. There is no dearth of extensive, informative and insightful literature on the subject. Historians conducted in-depth research on Indian workers living in several sugar colonies which includes Mauritius, British Guinea, Trinidad, Jamaica, Dutch Guiana (Suriname), Areneda, French Guiana, St. Vincent, Fiji and other colonies of Africa. A majority of historians have observed emigration of indentured labourers from India in the context of the pull factors, while some have relied on a combination of both pull and push factors.

This book presents the results of a study that relies purely on the push factors and is a supply-side analysis of migration under two different systems of recruitment—colonial and internal. It is a study of the circumstances within the country under which Indian labourers went to sugar colonies when a demand for replacement labour was raised by the planters of those sugar colonies as a consequence of the abolition of slave trade, slavery and the Emancipation Act of 1833. The study also analyses the circumstances that resulted in a reduction in colonial requirement for labour and the rise of industrialization in India, and how the push factor became an interstate phenomenon that induced these said labourers to change their route inside the country. Thus the focus of the book is on the supply mechanism, i.e. the push factor, which greatly influenced the migratory transition of Indians during the period between 1842 and 1900.

The book is divided into two parts. Part I, which is further divided into two chapters, examines the background of the colonial history of emigration from India and reviews the colonial economic conditions, the pattern of colonial requirements and also the terms and conditions that have emerged from both sides: the colonies and India. The first chapter introduces the book providing historical facts and figures related to certain circumstances, especially the origination of emigration. Also, the reason behind Calcutta Port gaining importance as a centre for embarkation has been explained in this chapter. The second chapter takes forward the discussion on the course of policies pursued by the Government of India regarding emigration.

Part II also consists of two chapters and gives a detailed analysis of the economic and social characteristics of the northern tract of India from where the largest number of people emigrated, and the area of importance under study. The third chapter discusses the rationale for emigration and examines the salient features related to these issues. It also covers the trend of internal migration from the some geographical region (where from people immigrated to sugar colonies) that arose due to an increased demand for labour with the growth and development of industries and plantation particularly in eastern India during the later periods of nineteenth century. The fourth chapter mainly focuses on the consequences of emigration and looks at the advantages and disadvantages experienced by the colonies and the emigration country that resulted from the large scale emigration over the course of the nineteenth century. At the end of each textual chapter, some original archival documents have been arranged is an organized manner in support of the illustrative explanations of the respective chapters.

In the final chapter major findings have been summarized. In the Appendices, various tables related to each chapter have been reproduced.

Sponsored by the Indian Council of Historical Research (ICHR), a revised report of which was submitted to the Council in 2006, the main purpose of the project was to search, collect, scrutinize, compile and edit quantitative and descriptive materials related to the emigration of Indians to the four 'sugar colonies'. The emigration of indentured labour started on an organized scale in 1842, coming to an end in 1900 following the gradual decline in demand for the Indian labourer. However, by this time, the said people had already started to settle in their own countries.

Sources of Data

An extensive research has been conducted in libraries and archives to discover statistical information on that class of population who emigrated for definite reasons and other specific circumstances. A thorough scrutiny of the rich collection of unpublished records on emigration data, available at the Directorate of State Archive of the Government of Bengal (commonly called as West Bengal State Archives at the Directorate of State Archive), was done. A study of the Parliamentary Papers publishing information on the material condition of the emigrants and the British Parliament's Legislation related to the Indian indentured labour system has also been analysed. In addition, information has been collected from published books and journals at both national and international levels.

Statistical Methodology

Statistical methodology used in this report has been confined mainly to ordinary tools like averages, frequency distribution, or proportional distribution over different variables like age, sex, caste, savings, mortality rate, etc., of emigrant people and the nature of their movement. The study is confined to more than half a century and the massive data related to the study has been handled with every care and a brief explanation has been discussed for the changes in every decade.

Different eminent scholars and surveyors at different periods have tried to analyse the reasons of emigration on the basis of available statistical data or from evidences, which have been utilized in this analysis. Since the study related to emigrants from Calcutta Port only, records of the various branches of the General Department of Government of Bengal, viz., (a) General, (b) Emigration, (c) Statistics, and (d) Miscellaneous, available at the State Archives of West Bengal, Kolkata are the main unpublished primary sources and have been used extensively.

Limitations

Due to scarcity of data and methodological inconsistencies in data collection, the study is marked by the following limitations:

1. Tables have been worked out mainly from unpublished data sources, which are not always readily available, and this limitation is responsible for irregularities in the statements showing emigration trends.
2. The study is not concerned with the whole long-term emigration period. Only the period 1842–1900 has been considered with the importance of the years from both ends.
3. Further, the method followed in collecting information or data is not known both for India as well as immigration colonies (except for census figures). So it is not possible to comment on the reliability of the data in most of the cases.
4. Finally, some statistical series are difficult to compare with others because of differences in data collection procedure, estimation techniques, methods applied and presentation.

SUTAPA DAS DHAR
CHANDRALEKHA BASU GHOSH

Acknowledgements

THE IDEA OF a project on the history of emigration from India over the nineteenth century fascinated us from two angles: it was interesting to study the actual circumstances under which emigration from India towards the plantation colonies emerged; and it was equally important to obtain knowledge of the reason behind changes in their destination at the end of the century. This book concentrates specifically on four sugar colonies where massive emigration took place, and the Calcutta Port through which the maximum number of emigrants embarked for the colonies.

The preparation of the report would not have been possible without the financial support and valuable assistance from different individuals and organizations: our deep gratitude goes to the authorities of ICHR for extending financial help in executing this interesting job and also their assistance towards publishing the book; we are also grateful to the Rabindra Bharati University, Kolkata, for granting us access to their facilities.

The book has deeply benefited from a generous supply of records of various departments of Government of West Bengal provided at the West Bengal State Archives (WBSA). Our gratitude is especially due to Dr Ananda Bhattacharya and Dr Bidisha Chakraborty at WBSA. We also wish to acknowledge our great debt to the staff of West Bengal Secretariat Library, National Library, Indian Statistical Institute and Centre for Studies in Social Sciences, Calcutta (CSSSC). They extended all kinds of help in supplying proceedings of General Department, official records, books, journals, etc., in time, which enriched the book giving it proper and integrated shape. In particular, we would like to express our gratitude to Asim Mukherjee, Assistant Librarian and Information Officer, National Library, Kolkata and Siddartha Sankar Roy, Librarian at CSSSC for providing us with not only information and documents but also invaluable advices. We are also thankful to Rita Sen Choudhury, the librarian of American Center, Kolkata, for her generous assistance in supplying us with some valuable documents that she collected from

USA on our demand. We would also like to thank Sasnik Paik, Assistant Librarian and Information Officer, National Library, who offered various assistances during our library works.

Our special thanks and love to Nilanjan Dhar, a young man of 22 years old, who has painted two beautiful images, one for the front cover of the book. We are also thankful to all our family members for giving us support and a constant inspiration in publishing of the book.

Finally, we wish to thank our husbands Biswanath Das, FCMA, and Prodyot Kumar Basu for their loving support and intellectual contributions whenever necessary.

The book is purely a research monograph and will be of value to people who are interested in continuing future research on a similar topic. It would give us great satisfaction if they find this volume useful. We undertake all responsibility for any shortcomings in the text.

SUTAPA DAS DHAR
CHANDRALEKHA BASU GHOSH

PART I

1

Colonial Emigration

INDIA HAS A long history of emigration. The nineteenth century is significant for large-scale emigration from India under the British rule. Generally, this trend of emigration to the Crown colonies, especially the sugar colonies was entirely uncontrolled. Therefore a useful starting point for understanding economic changes and become migration associated with sugar industries in Mauritius and other Caribbean countries is to analyse some of the most important political and economic factors that are responsible for this form of labour emigration from India.

The early decades of British Rule (1810–1968) in Mauritius witnessed great confusion over the terms and conditions of the capitulations signed by the French leaders who had surrendered the island to Britain. Sir Robert Farquhar, the first Governor of Mauritius appointed by the British in 1810, faced serious problems in tackling the crisis over British-owned territory. The development of British plantation was largely supported by the large manual workforce which Europeans managed by taking advantage of the slave trade in Africa. But with the upsurge of abolitionists in the Americas and Europe, the trade of slaves was abolished in the British Empire through the abolition of Slave Trade Act in 1807. British authorities anticipated serious shortage of labour. Sir Farquhar's duty was to uphold British authority and ensure compliance with British law. This also included the Abolition Act of 1807, which made the importation of slaves into British territories illegal. At the same time, he found a grave shortage of labour. Enforcing the Abolition Act meant banning the supply of slaves, which, he thought, was disastrous for the country's economy. In order to please both the British government and the planters, he asked for a temporary postponement of the execution of the law in a despatch to Lord Liverpool, the Secretary of State for the Colonies, in February 1811. However, his effort was a total failure. At that time, all the proprietors were French and the labour force was made up entirely of slaves, the Malagasy and Africans. According to the tax rolls, there were 60,000 slaves in Mauritius.[1]

The anti-slavery movement among the British population, and their victory in 1834, led to a long period of crisis throughout the colonies that were dependent on slave trade. 'The Emancipation Act of 1833, passed by Parliament made the liberated slaves "apprentice" to their old masters for six years.'[2] The apprentice class was employed in agriculture or in agricultural based industry. 'The shortage of agricultural labour arising out of the virtual refusal of the liberated slaves to work in the sugar plantations of Mauritius, British Guiana, Trinidad, and Jamaica threatened the existence of the sugar industries there.'[3] The planters took up various methods to: (i) increase the output from the labourers and (ii) insure the flow of labour. 'One such method was the employment of "apprentices" on Saturdays'.[4] The period of apprenticeship was full of conflict between the liberated slaves and their former masters. The slaves felt that they had been deceived and began to work or leave plantations according to their will. The working of the apprentice system thus effected did not last long and in April 1838, the question of an early termination of the 'apprenticeship' system arose.

The council of the government in Mauritius was not interested in an early termination of the system. However, due to the spread of the emancipation movement, particularly in the British West Indies, it was impossible to continue with the institution in Mauritius. Mauritian planters expected the serious effect of the Emancipation Act as early as 1834. And it is believed that between August 1834 and May 1837, at least 7,000 emigrants left Calcutta for Mauritius.[5] Thus, in anticipation and 'with the permission of the Government, they [the planters] had begun to recruit and import Indian workers at their own expense, and by the end of 1838, there were about 25,000 Indian workers on the island'.[6]

Planters of large West Indian colonies, viz., British Guiana, Trinidad and Jamaica, had also realized that with the expiry of the six-year period of apprenticeship, the continuous supply of labourers—necessary for the cultivation of sugar cane and operation of sugar mills—would be severely hampered. 'The planters also realized that missionaries would encourage the emancipated blacks to demand wages befitting a free man. . . .'[7] And in view of these alarming prospects, in 1836, John Gladstone, the father of British statesman William Ewart Gladstone, and owner of the two estates in British Guiana (Vreed-en-Hoop and Vreed-en-Stein), made an inquiry about the possibility of getting an alternative source of their future labour supply. In search of this, in 1834, he inquired to the Calcutta recruiting firm Messrs Gellanders Arbuthnot and Company 'if it would be possible to get about one hundred Bengalees—the same type as that company has been sending to Mauritius for light work in the fields, the mills and the distilleries in Demerara'.[8] At that time, the Indian government had no cause to interfere in recruiting labourers to colonies. With the contract of five years of indenture under the provision of the British Guiana Masters and Servants Ordinance of 22 June 1836, and the return passages of indentured coolies to the port or place of indenture in India being guaranteed, John Gladstone joined a group of other planters in signing a contract, which complied a firm of Liverpool merchants to supply them two shiploads of coolies. Thus, the first immigration to British Guiana from India started in 1838 and the two vessels, the *Whitby*, with 246 emigrants, and the *Hesperus*, with 168 emigrants, embarked from Calcutta and reached British Guiana on 6 May 1838.[9]

Emigration through the Calcutta Port started much before 1842. However, during the period between 1834 and 1839, emigration was through private operators and there were reports of various abuses against the emigrants. Details on abuses will be discussed in Chapter 2. In 1839, however, the Government of India was forced to suspend the operation due to various reports of such repression and abuses. The system resumed only three years later, when British Prime Minister Robert Real directed the Government of India to re-open the operation of emigration under proper safeguards. In 1842, the new state-controlled emigration from India to Mauritius began, but the ban on emigration to West Indies continued up to 1845. After the Government of India Act XXI of 16 November 1844 permitted emigration to the colonies of British Guiana, Jamaica and Trinidad from the Calcutta Port and Madras Port, the government started to export coolies to these colonies.

After the prohibition on emigration of coolies from India was withdrawn in 1843, the demand for labour from Calcutta and Madras were: 5,000 in British Guiana, 5,000 in Jamaica and 2,500 in Trinidad, although the initial demand was for only 5,000 labourers—2,000 each for Jamaica and British Guiana and 1,000 for Trinidad, the three renowned colonies of British West Indies.[10] No serious objections were raised to this request and the emigration agents, Thomas Caird at Calcutta and Captain Wilson at Madras, were each directed to recruit one-half of the 12,500 coolies authorized for the initial season of 1844–5. Emigration continued until 1848 when it was temporarily suspended. During that period, 21,791 coolies were dispatched from Calcutta and Madras. Of that number, British Guiana received 11,888; Trinidad, 5403; and Jamaica, 4,500.[11]

Mauritius recruited the highest number of low-waged labour force from India, but the cost of emigration was high. The pinch of this financial pressure necessarily required a supply of permanent rather than temporary labour, which was possible only if emigration of the women and families of Indian labourers could be encouraged. 'Most of the labourers signed up as single men; if they were married they left wives and children in the care of the elders of their joint family.'[12] The total demand for plantation labour in Mauritius was 30,000. In 1843, G.F. Dick, the Colonial Secretary of Mauritius , in a letter to C. Anderson, the Acting Protector of Emigrants, expressed the view of the Colonial Authority on the subject of immigration to the island, when he writes,

The extent of immigration is a point upon which the authority of India may not have any well defined information and may have been led to apprehend that it was required on a much more extended scale than, as you are aware, is necessary here. With 30,000 labourers it may be calculated that the island will, for the present, be well supplied with hands, and that after that number shall have been introduced, immigration will be required only to meet the reduction that will take place by labourers returning to their native land and ordinary mortality, not exceeding in all probability, 1,500 or 2,000 annually.[13]

Anderson's mission was to give sufficient information about the supply of annual number of labourers from India required at Mauritius along with special effort to encourage women from India to emigrate. Based on an official return from the Emigration Office of India, he sent sufficient information about the number of Indian emigrants that was expected to reach Mauritius from the three ports of India, Calcutta, Bombay and Madras, by 1 January 1844 (Table 1.1).[14] His estimation was to receive about 29,000 emigrants out of which 2,700 women and 700 children. The estimate thus made by him is given in tabular form (Table 1.1).

TABLE 1.1:   Number of Emigrants to Mauritius from Calcutta, Madras, Bombay, 1843

Emigration from	Number of Emigrants	Percentage of Emigrants
Calcutta—Reached	13,679	47.69
—Expected to Reach by 20 November	2,500	08.72
TOTAL	16,179	56.41
Madras	11,000	38.36
Bombay	1,500	05.23
GRAND TOTAL	28,679	100.00

Source: Parliamentary Papers, vol. XXXV, 1844, p. 234.

In 1849, Rene Kuczynski, a famous British colonial demographer, reported that after a number of ordinances were passed in Mauritius in 1842, and suspension of emigration from Calcutta to Mauritius was withdrawn, 'In 1843 there [Mauritius] came not fewer than 34,525. From 1843 to 1866 the arrivals numbered 339,706 and the departures 84,949. After that, immigration became smaller.'[15]

In 1842, only 459 emigrants embarked from Calcutta Port to Mauritius, and 3,738 labourers went to the three West Indian sugar colonies from Calcutta Port in 1845, according to official sources (Appendix I).

Thus, coolie emigration, which began as a privately conducted enterprise in 1838, became a state-controlled system from 1842; and after a number of terms and contracts between the Government of India and the sugar colonies, the export of coolies from India had taken a definite form by around 1870.

George A. Grierson's report of 1883 is one of the most comprehensive study of Indian emigration in the nineteenth century. The table formulated by him showing the names of colonies and the number of coolies who had emigrated from India up to 1882 clearly depicted that emigration took place largely to four sugar colonies, viz., Mauritius, British Guiana, Trinidad, and Jamaica (Table 1.2).

Mauritius, due to her proximity to India—where abundance of comparatively cheap labourers were available—imported the highest number of coolies throughout the period, 1842–1900. Demerara was

TABLE 1.2: The Colonies and the Number of
Indian Population, 1882

	Colonies	Approximate Number of Indian Population
	Mauritius	248,000
	Larger West Indian Islands:	
Under British Possession	(a) Demerara	88,000
	(b) Trinidad	51,000
	(c) Jamaica	11,000
	SUB-TOTAL	398,000
	Total of smaller West Indian Islands	31,400
Total under British Possession		429,400
Total under Foreign Possession		77,043
Total Coolie population in all colonies		506,443

Source: Computed from Grierson, 1883, p. 2.

next to Mauritius in demand for coolie labour. Jamaica imported least coolies due to its own large population, and growing opposition to coolie emigration in the colony—which lasted until a considerable later date.

Table 1.2 clearly shows that the four sugar colonies—Mauritius, Demerara, Trinidad and Jamaica—were destinations for more than three-fourths, i.e. 79 per cent, of the 506,443 coolie population from British India.

Calcutta Port: The Most Important Zone of Recruitment

Indian emigration took place only through three distinct zones of recruitment around Calcutta, Madras and Bombay, with Calcutta recruiting the greatest numbers and Bombay the least. A statistical study of gross emigration from India including a comparison with emigration through the Calcutta Port to the four sugar colonies clearly establishes the fact that for many years labour migrated largely through the Calcutta Port (Appendix I). The most probable reason behind this was that the labourers who went through this port were familiar with fieldwork, which the colonies mostly preferred.

The emigration process from India to sugar colonies worked both upon push and pull factors, but relied mainly on the push factors. According to the Royal Commission in India, 1931, 'Emigration has always arisen mainly from the difficulty of finding an adequate livelihood in one's native place and this is the predominant force which impels the Indian villager to seek industrial employment.'[16] People migrated overseas from India 'mainly from the most overcrowded agricultural districts of India where crop failure could plunge sections of the village community into near starvation'.[17] From a close scrutiny of the observed figures for departure from India emerges a clear correlation between the departed Indians and the natural disasters that primarily befell in the North-Western Provinces (present Uttar Pradesh), Bihar and Orissa during the period 1860–1, 1865–6 or 1873–5.

British land revenue policies in India were largely responsible for millions of unemployed in India during the late eighteenth and early nineteenth centuries.[18] These policies caused increased landless peasants and North India was most affected. J. Scoble, secretary for the Committee of the British and Foreign Anti-Slavery Society disclosed the fact that '. . . persons are inveigled from the interior under false pretences, held in a kind of imprisonment in Calcutta, and smuggled on boardship; the whole pasiness being conducted by duffadens, or crimps, and being nothing short of systematic kidnapping . . .'.[19] Under these factors, the Calcutta Port naturally became an important hub of recruitment and boarding station for emigrants.

The Calcutta Port first gained significance when the Mauritius government requested for emigrants from India only through the said port. In the early years of the 1840s and 1850s, labourers to Mauritius and British Guiana were largely from the Chotonagpur Plateau, the 'Hill Coolies'. 'But the number of aboriginals gradually decreased, partly from the competition of the tea districts, partly because of the heavy mortality at sea among this class of emigrants.'[20] However in the period 1857–9 (the Indian mutiny years) the highest rates of emigration of Indian workers from Calcutta to Mauritius occurred. The cause behind this increase was partly due to the rise in global sugar prices and a consequent increase in sugar cultivation, when Emigration Agent received instructions from the Colonial Authorities to send as many labourers to Port Louis as he could collect. This demand coincided with the disturbances within the country during the same period due to Indian uprising which worked well as a push factor causing a large influx of rural population of the disturbed districts to emigrate, particularly the people of Shahabad and Ghazeepore (see supporting document at the end of this chapter, Gen Dept., 20 October 1859), a region which is closely linked to massive recruitment of sepoys.[21]

The Court of Directors of the East India Company proposed a copy of Act XXI of 1843—formulated to regulate the emigration of labourers from India to Mauritius. The purpose of the Act was to secure a permanent rather than a temporary and unsettled immigration. The Emigration Agent appointed by the Governor of Mauritius was authorized to control emigration, which, from 1 January 1844, was restricted to the Calcutta Port. Thus, the business of procuring emigrants had been taken out of the hands of private agents and given exclusively to an officer acting on behalf of the government of Mauritius.[22] The importance of the Act was that it would confine future emigration within certain limits and protect the real interests of an ignorant people thereof and that the Calcutta Port alone would be able to furnish sufficient emigrants. The Act also considered the point that emigration from a single port would be less expensive and easier to oversee than to carry out emigration operations from more than one port.

Like Mauritius, West Indian colonies also expressed interest in acquiring sufficient number of emigrants from Calcutta, principally because of the inferior grade of the Indian natives sent from Madras in the 1840s. 'A composite of the yearly totals issued by the land and emigration commissioners discloses that between 1851 and 1870 British Guiana imported 67,616 coolies. . . . A total of 40,000 came to Trinidad from India during the same period. . . . Over the same number of years Jamaica imported 10,554 coolies. . . .'[23] Thus, an overwhelming majority of labourers were sent from Calcutta to the West Indian colonies during 1851–70.

Notes

1. Moses D.E. Nwulia, *The History of Slavery in Mauritius and the Seychelles, 1810–1875*, London: Associated University Press, 1981, p. 41.
2. Panchanan Saha, *Emigration of Indian Labour (1834–1800)*, Delhi: People's Publishing House, 1970, p. 6.
3. Ibid., p. 1.
4. Nwulia, *The History of Slavery*, p. 150.
5. Great Britain, J. Geoghegan, Esq., Under Secretary to the Government of India, *Notes on Emigration from India*, Parliamentary Papers (hereafter PP), vol. XLVII, Paper 314, 1874, p. 2.
6. Nwulia, *The History of Slavery*, p. 181.
7. Edgar L. Erickson, 'The Introduction of East Indian Coolies into the British West Indies', *The Journal of Modern History*, vol. 6, no. 2, June 1934, p. 128.
8. Ibid., p. 128.
9. Erickson, 'The Introduction of East Indian Coolies', p. 130.
10. Ibid., p. 137.
11. Ibid., pp. 137–8.
12. For a full account of the importance of introducing 'women and families' for overseas emigration, see PP, vol. XXXV, 1844, p. 233; and also Tinker Huge, *The Banyan Tree: Overseas Emigrants from India, Pakistan and Bangladesh*, London: Oxford University Press (hereafter OUP), 1977, p. 4.
13. Great Britain, *Emigration of Indian Labourers to the Mauritius*, PP, vol. XXXV, 1844, p. 233.
14. Ibid., p. 234.
15. R.R. Kuczynski, *Demographic Survey of British Colonial Empire* (issued under the auspices of the Royal Institute of International Affairs), vol. II, London and New York: OUP, 1949, p. 797.
16. Great Britain, *Report of the Royal Commission in India 1931*, London. Published by his Majesty's Stationary Office 1931, p. 14.
17. Tinker Huge, *A New System of Slavery: The Export of Indian Labour Overseas*, Oxford, London: OUP (Published for the Institute of Race Relations), 1974, p. 119.
18. Ron Ramdin, *Arising from Bondage: A History of the Indo-Caribbean People*, London: I.B. Tauris Publishers, 2000, p. 11.
19. Great Britain, *Emigration of Indian Labourers to the Mauritius*, PP, vol. xxxv, 1844, p. 231.
20. Great Britain, J. Geoghegan, Esq., Under Secretary to the Government of India, *Notes on Emigration from India*, PP, vol. XLVII, 1874, p. 71.

21. Tinker Huge, *The Banyan Tree: Overseas Emigrants from India, Pakistan and Bangladesh,* London: OUP, 1977, p. 4.
22. Great Britain, *Emigration of Indian Labourers to the Mauritius,* PP, vol. XXXV, 1844, p. 232.
23. Erickson, 'The Introduction of East Indian Coolies', p. 146.

SUPPORTING DOCUMENTS

Proceedings, General Department, 20th October 1859

[No.23]   From   Captain Thomas Hill, for Protector of Emigrants at Calcutta
               To   Lord H.U. Browne, Under Secretary to the Government of Bengal (No. 3 dated the 8th October, 1859)

I have the honour . . . regarding the great increase in the Emigration of coolies from Calcutta to Mauritius and requesting a Report upon the probable cause which have led to this increase.

The increase dates from the early part of the year 1857, about which time the Emigration Agent received instructions from the Colonial Authorities to send as many labourers to Port Louis as he could collect. About the same period the country became disturbed, and the rural population took advantage to leave their disturbed Districts and emigrate, particularly the people of Shahabad, as will be seen by the synopses of the Records entered marginally.

The disposition to emigrate has unquestionably been kept alive and fostered by the Recruiters under Mauritius Ordinance No. 30 of 1858 under the influence of private agency.

In 1857, 9,846 adults were embarked of which—

2,229 came from Shahabad
1,658 came from Ghazeepore &
1,388 came from Sahebgunge

In 1858–59, 20,166 adults were embarked of which—

5,522 came from Shahabad
2,921 came from Ghazeepore &
3,378 came from Sahebgunge

Proceedings, General Department, Emigration Department, January 1862

[No. 6]   From   W.F. Fergussan, Esq. Secy, Landholder's and Commercial Association
               To   E.H. Lushington, Esq, Secy to the Government of Bengal (dated the 30th December, 1861)

The Committee of the Association having taken into consideration the present system of coolies Emigration from this Port view with alarm the strenuous efforts which are being made by the various Agencies established in Calcutta, for the encouragement of native Emigration to the West Indies, Mauritius and the French Colonies of Bourbon.

They have further noticed that a Joint Stock Company has been lately established for the growth of cotton in Australia, the prominent feature of which is the importation of labour from India.

An erroneous impression appear to exists in these various Colonies, and in England, that India is overpopulated, whereas except in very few Districts the contrary is the case.

It is an admitted fact that the price of labour has within the last few years risen fully 50 per cent and the cost in the construction of Railways, and other public works now in progress in the vicinity of Calcutta, over and above the estimates will prove this.

Some of the vast tracts of uncultivated lands amounting to millions of acres, as detailed in the returns published by the Supreme Government, much of which is fitted for the cultivation of Cotton, Tea, Coffee, and Cereals, will it is presumed, be applied for by Europeans under the liberal and encouraging Rules laid down by His Excellency the Governor General in his Minute of the 17th October, sanctioning the acquisition of freeholds on India, but this boon will be deprived of much of the advantage it should yield; if at the same time the Home Government and other Countries in taking away the labour that is available.

2

Sugar Colonies

Economic Conditions and Rules
Relating to Emigration

Economy of Four Sugar Colonies and their
Requirement for Labour Importation

D URING THE NINETEENTH CENTURY, British Guiana, Trinidad
and Jamaica, the three sugar colonies in the West Indies, had
different commercial histories. Situated within the tropical
region, the three colonies had similar climatic conditions and the produce
of the soil was favourable for plantation of sugar cane, which was the staple
crop in the whole region. The colonies grew other products as well: while
coffee was cultivated in all three colonies, on the hillsides, Jamaica also
grew ginger and pimento; Trinidad cultivated cocoa on a large scale during
the 1870s; and British Guiana grew cotton. Still, sugar remained the most
extensive industry for the West Indies during the nineteenth century. The
industry was based on two pillars—slave labour and protection.[1]

Although these colonies produced one great staple—subject to tropical
climatic conditions—and had a common interest as a whole, each colony
had its own peculiar characteristics.

The colony of British Guiana—popularly known among East Indians
as Demerara—was created in 1831 when Demerara, Essequibo and
Berbice, three separate colonies, were combined and their administration
conducted from Georgetown. Located at the northern end of South
America, the colony was the largest in area, and intersected by wonderful
rivers, but the interior region is little known and only partially explored.
Only a narrow area of land along the coast, approximately 1,750 sq. mi.,
was cultivated and chiefly occupied by the sugar industry.[2]

Trinidad is situated in the southernmost part of the chain of West
Indian islands. 'Of its estimated area of 1,287,600 acres, about 213,292
were appropriated of which only 53,000 acres were under cultivation. The

rest was Crown Land.'[3] Trinidad was a new island settlement compared to Jamaica, and most attractive to planters.

Jamaica was the most fertile of the colonies. It is the largest island of the Caribbean and situated in the far north-west of the West Indies. After British occupation, the effect of the changes principally brought about by imperial legislation appeared to be more striking in Jamaica and British Guinea. The colony produced its largest quantity, i.e. 150,000 hogsheads of sugar, in 1805. Gradually over four decades, production dropped mainly due to emancipation of slaves in 1833 and at the termination of the apprenticeship system in 1838, when the British planters felt the need of an alternative source of labour in the sugar plantations for continuation of production. By the time the sugar legislation was passed in 1846, production had fallen to 36,000 hogsheads. In 1829, the exports of British Guiana were 66,772 hogsheads of sugar, 6,778,350 pounds of coffee and 7,272 bales of cotton. In 1839, the sugar production of the colony fell to 38,443 hogsheads. 1849 saw a further reduction with 32,000 hogsheads of sugar, 91,056 pounds of coffee, while cotton cultivation entirely vanished.[4]

The power of production of an estate largely depends upon the amount spent in draining, good cultivation, houses, hospitals, cottages, boiling houses and sugar machinery. However, thousands of pounds are required for their establishment.

Acute shortage of labour in the early nineteenth century brought sugar estates in all parts of the West Indies to ruin. The interests of the West Indian planters were affected by three major changes in their economy, which led them to take protection. Those changes were related to the improvement in technology, the emancipation of slaves and the development of beet sugar.

At the beginning of the century the West Indian industry was established on the basis of the small scale 'estate', using animals for transportation and often for power, boiling the cane juice in open 'coppers'. Improved techniques and new machinery were introduced gradually throughout the century—central factories, vacuum and centrifugal processes in refining, steam power and tramways. But these changes came first to new areas of sugar production, and this development called for a complete renovation of the West Indian sugar industry if it were to continue to compete in a world market. A second challenge was presented by the emancipation of the slaves throughout the British Empire during the 1830's. In this case the problem was one of social readjustment and reorganization of the labour system on a free basis. Finally the development of beet sugar, which became increasingly important from the 1870s onwards, introduced a new source of competition for all cane sugar producers.[5]

The imposition of protective duties on foreign sugar and the complete prohibition of slave-grown foreign sugar eliminated competition in the British markets. British mercantile houses used to supply not only credit but also slaves and other necessities to the planters. Thus, 'a protective duty on sugar at home, abundance of capital (compensation for slavery), and the high price of sugar in the European markets made it possible for planters to import labour from other countries.'[6]

The island of Mauritius, situated in the South Indian Ocean about 1,500 mi. from the East Coast of Africa, covers an area of about 716 sq. mi. Sugar was the sole industry in the island of Mauritius and constituted 98 per cent of its exports. Thus, the whole economic life of the island revolved around this industry.[7]

Like the West Indian colonies, the prosperity of Mauritius was completely dependent on the cultivation and manufacture of sugar from the very beginning of the nineteenth century. Sugar production in the island increased from 1 million lb in 1809 to above 24 million lb. in 1824, but the colony's production was far below capacity due to the imposition of a differential sugar duty. In 1823, this duty was equalized with the sugar of the British plantations, which resulted in a tremendous increase in the production of sugar in Mauritius. Sugar production rose to 68 million lb. in 1830 and, by 1832, to 73 million lb. and had a wholesome effect on its public revenue. This equalization brought a large influx of British capital, which was mostly invested in sugar mill machinery.[8] However, the influx of indentured labourers from India and their capacity to hard work brought a big fillip to the sugar industry in Mauritius in the following decade, which is reflected in the export figures in Table 2.1. Thus, for planters of both West Indies and Mauritius, with the decline

TABLE 2.1: Statement showing Sugar Exports from Mauritius during the Period 1846–52

Year	Quantity of sugar exported (French lbs.)
1846	122,494,822
1847	114,525,743
1848	110,989,017
1849	126,678,577
1850	110,937,388
1851	133,329,092
1852	141,639,662

Source: Nwulia, 1981, p. 188 (quoted from Report of the Finance Committee, 13 August 1853. C.O. 170/37).

of other plantations, only the cultivation of sugar remained profitable towards which most of the labour shifted.

Inducement to Emigration
Terms and Conditions

The system of immigration to other colonies from India passed through several inquiries and considerations, and many valuable reforms were introduced throughout the period by the Government of India as well as the colonial offices.

During the first phase of emigration, which extended from 1834 to 1839, the only measure of control that the government attempted to exercise was that the emigrants were required to appear before a magistrate in order to convince him regarding their freedom of choice and the knowledge of the conditions that they had accepted. Labour contracts were valid for five years and wages were Rs.5 per month, in addition to liberal rations and clothing.[9]

However, as stated earlier in the previous chapter, this phase of emigration was arranged privately, and Indian emigrants were abused by the agents in the conduct of the emigration from India to Mauritius, and as a consequence, suspended. The report of the committee appointed in Calcutta to enquire into the matter agreed with this allegation and opposed further emigration. The report stated that 'very grave abuses had prevailed in India, emigrants having been, in too many cases, entrapped by force and fraud, and systematically plundered of nearly six months' wages, nominally advanced to them, but really divided, on pretences more or less transparent, among the predacious crew engaged in the traffic'.[10] Sir J.P. Grant, one of the members of the committee, recommended some measures, which included the restriction of emigration to certain ports with some proper safeguards. He suggested for some procedures like appointing a protector for Indian Immigrant to eliminate the element of force on unwilling emigrants. British parliament in 1842 approved his proposal which appears to lead to the second phase of emigration, in 1842, from India to Mauritius and to other colonies of the West Indies in 1845.

In the 1870s, the rules relating to emigration from the Calcutta Port were undertaken by the Governor General of India in Council to guide J.G. Grant, the protector of emigrants, towards duties to emigrants and also to guide the medical inspector over the state of sanitation of the emigration depot and the emigrants.

Several terms of contract for emigrants to each colony were also undertaken by the colony. In order to make the emigrants aware of the terms and conditions and prospects in the different colonies, printed copies of notice in English, Urdu and Devanagari language meant for the coolies were forwarded by the emigration agents of several colonies to the protector of emigrants in Calcutta. The terms offered to prospective emigrants by several colonies are given in tabular form. From the Table 2.2, it is observed that labourers who migrated to the four colonies obtained the following benefits with respect to each colony:

1. West Indian colonies provided return passages to the emigrants, while Mauritius did not.
2. Mauritius supplied ration for the whole indentured period, but West Indian colonies lacked in this advantage.
3. Rate of wages was higher for West Indian colonies and paid on a weekly basis, whereas in Mauritius, the rate was lower and paid on a monthly basis.
4. Regarding working hours, Demerara provided more privilege with seven working hours as compared to other colonies, which demanded nine hours of fieldwork.

Notes

1. Panchanan Saha, *Emigration of Indian Labour (1834–1900)*, Delhi: People's Publishing House, 1970, p. 5.
2. Ron Ramdin, *Arising from Bondage: A History of the Indo-Caribbean People*, London: I.B. Tauris Publishers, 2000, p. 51.
3. Ibid., p. 77.
4. Government of Bengal, Nevil Lubbock, *Present Position of the West India Colonies*, Read at a meeting of the Royal Colonial Institute, London, General Department, Emigration Branch, July 1877, pp. 2–3. WBSA, Kolkata.
5. P.D. Curtin, 'Sugar Prices and West Indian Prosperity', *The Journal of Economic History*, vol. XIV, no. 2, 1954, p. 158.
6. Saha, *Emigration of Indian Labour*, p. 12, Collected from Legislative Department (Emigration) nos. 4–13, 6 March 1837.
7. S. Ridley, *Report on the Condition of Indians in Mauritius*, New Delhi: Manager, Government of India Press, 1940, pp. 2–3.
8. Saha, *Emigration of Indian Labour*, pp. 2–3, Collected from Home Public (Emigration) Department, no. 12, 1845.
9. Great Britain, Sanderson Commission, *Report of the Committee on Emigration from India to the Crown Colonies & Prolectorates*, PP, vol. XXVII, 1910.
10. Great Britain, J. Geoghegan, Notes on Emigration from India, PP, vol. XLVII, paper 314, 1874, p. 6.

SUPPORTING DOCUMENTS

Parliamentary Papers, House of Commons, Vol. 45, 1847

Enclosures in No. 4

Memorandum

The position of the Colony is at the moment most deplorable; bankruptcy and want stare everyone in the face and an extensive abandonment of estates appears inevitable after the present crop, unless bold and immediate measures of relief speedily afforded.

Properly regulated immigration is essential to the ultimate propensity of Trinidad, but the immediate and pressing demand is for money; fresh capital is required to maintain estates and to revivify the enormous sums that have been expended in sugar cultivation for the last seven or eight years; without this all will be sunk, which will consummate the utter ruin of the planter, the failure of the emancipation experiment and entail starvation on the labouring population of the economy.

Proceedings, General Department, March 1859

[No. 106] From   Surgeon Major P.W.D. Commins, M.D., Protector of
                 Emigrants, Calcutta
          To   The Secretary to the Government of Bengal, General
                 Department

I have every reason to believe that there are many private Depot in and about Calcutta and Raneegunge which is entirely at variance with the orders of Government, there being a public Depot at Bhawanipore, where all Emigrants should be lodged.

I would respectfully suggest that Magistrate of Calcutta, 24-Parganas and Raneegunge be requested to enquire and report upon the matter, as I have every reason to believe that the people collected in these private Depots are misled and have not a fair opportunity of knowing the particulars about Emigration—many of them being brought to Calcutta for embarkation only a day or two previous to the date arranged for the vessels sailing and although my Assistant gives them every information he possibly can, and asked them if they are willing Emigrants, they reply in the affirmative, being told to do so by the Native Recruiters.

Proceedings, General Department,
September 1871, Page 2

[No. 7]   From   F.O. Mayne, Esq. C.B., Commissioner of the Allahabad
                 Division
          To   C.A. Elliot, Esq., Officiating Secretary to the Government of
                 NWPs (No. 188, dated Allahabad, the 24th July 1871)

I have the honour to submit, for the information and orders of Government, a letter No. 86, dated 19th instant, with enclosure, from the magistrate of Allahabad, reporting an important case of infringement of the Indian Emigration Act (VII of 1871) together with a copy of my orders in reply.

In the first place the Protector of Emigrants under section 16 may license so many fit persons as to him seem necessary to be recruiters of labourers. The persons they employ for the purpose often come from a distance upcountry, and it naturally follows that the Protector of Emigrants in Calcutta can know very little about them, and it is quite possible that unscrupulous men of bad character may unwillingly be enlisted in this service. In my opinion no recruiter in any place other than in the Presidency towns should be licensed until the magistrate of the district where he ordinarily resides shall pronounce him to be a fit person.

Secondly, with knowledge of the ignorant people amongst whom the recruiter is thrown, and of how easily they are duped, the expediency of a recruiter wearing a badge under section 20 is very questionable. . . . I think no badge should be worn by either recruiter or agent.

Thirdly, I agree with Mr. Robertson that depots for coolies should only be allowed at the headquarters of a district, where they can be controlled by the magistrate of the district, and that over every such depot shall be affixed a board on which shall be printed in large letters in English, Urdu and Hindee—'Emigrants Recruiting Depot for the Mautitius' (or other places as the case may be).

Fourthly, I think it is also advisable that the police should be given a list of all such depots, . . . and that a police officer, not under the rank of an inspector, should visit each depot daily, . . . for the purpose of seeing that no persons are detained against their will.

Finally, recruiters should be allowed to employ as agents only such persons as are approved by the magistrate of the district.

I would not abolish recruiters, but I would place them and their agent more immediately under control and with some such rules as I have suggested above. . . .

Apparently the only form of register prescribed under section 27, Act VII of 1871, in use, is that which has hitherto obtained under Act XIII of 1864.

Proceedings, General Department, Emigration Branch, December 1872

[No. 17] Condition and Prospect of Indian Emigrants in the Colonies
No. 65 dated Calcutta, the 15th June 1872.

From H.A. Firth, Esq., Emigration Agent for British Guiana, Calcutta
To   Dr. J.G. Garrow Grant, Protector of Emigrants, Calcutta

I now forward printed copy of notice to coolies intending to emigrate to British Guiana, which I hope you will submit to the Lieutenant Governor of Bengal without delay.

I will in a few days send you a supply of these notices printed on strong paper in English, Urdu and Davanagari.

NOTICE

To Coolies Intending to Emigrate to British Guiana, generally called Demerara

Journey to Calcutta	You will be taken free of expense to Calcutta, and while
In Calcutta	You will be well fed and properly lodged until the ship sails, and should you be ill, the greatest care will be taken of you
Voyage	When the ship is ready you will be supplied with good clothing. The finest ships are selected, and the voyage takes from two to three months. The food, medicines, and other appliances on board, are of good quality; and your health, comfort, and safety, will be most carefully attended to. The India Govt. has appointed officers who are most strict and vigilant in securing for you all these advantages.
Arrival in Demerara	On your arrival in Demerara, there are Government officials
Government Protection	On purpose to advise and protect you, and at all times during your residence there are greatest care and watchfulness is exercised by the Government of Demerara is seeing that all your rights and privileges are secured to you, whether in health or in sickness.
Religion	Your religion is in no way interfered with, and both Hindoos and Mahomedans are protected alike.
Indian Population	You will find upwards of 40,000 of your countrymen comfortably settled on the sugar plantations in Demerara, besides many more in towns and villages.
House	You will have a good house, rent free, to live in and the Protector of Immigrants in Demerara will take care that you are not overcrowded or separated from your relatives.
Garden	You will have plenty of garden grand to cultivate at your leisure.
Climate, water, fruits, vegetables	The climate of Demerara is never so hot or so cold as in India, and suits your countrymen; and you will find an abundance of fresh water, fruits and vegetables.
Letters and remittances	If you wish to write or to remit money to your friends in India, the Protector will always be glad to direct you in sending such letters or money orders through the agent here.
Work, Amount of Wages	You will be required to cultivate sugar cane, and to make sugar, rum and molasses. Great varieties of work, either for strong men or for women and children, are always

abundantly available, and the amount of money earned depends on the strength and experience of the labour. Upwards of eighty lacs of rupees are paid yearly as wages to different classes of labourers; certain work is done by the day, but most is ticca or task work. An able-bodied industrious man easily earns ten annas in about 6 hours, women and children in proportion.

Cattle, Jewellery, Bank deposits, Return to India

Your countrymen in Demerara own livestock worth upwards of thirteen lacs of rupees, jewellery worth six lacs of rupees, besides money in the savings bank, and other properties amounting to nearly thirty lacs of rupees. After five years industrial residence you may return to India, at your own expense, or if you re-indenture for another five years you will receive a present of Rs.104. Nearly five lacs of rupees are thus paid yearly to coolies, which is in addition to their wages. After ten years you are entitled to a free passage back to India. Nearly seven thousand of your countrymen returned in sixteen years, bringing with them over twelve and half lacs of rupees in cash, besides valuable jewellery.

Females

Females will find immense advantages. Those who are married will be fully protected, and those who wish to marry will have excellent offer from their well-to-do countrymen. Throughout British Guiana the women are generally laden with gold or silver ornaments. Females when pregnant or suckling children are not required to work.

Calcutta
11th June 1872

H.A. Firth
Emigration Agent for British Guiana

Proceedings, General Department, Emigration Branch, March 1873

[No. 30] Department of Agriculture, Revenue and Commerce, Calcutta, the 19th February 1873

Notification

The following rules relating to emigration from the port of Calcutta have been made by the Governor General in Council under the provisions of section 56 of the Indian Emigration Act, 1871 and are hereby published for general information:

Rules for the Guidance of the Protector of Emigrants

1. The attention of the Protector of Emigrants is directed to those sections of the Act which define his position and duties, the position and duties of others who are engaged under the Act, and to the following rules.

2. Besides the usual reports [under section 8 of the Act] on return emigrants, the treatment they have experienced on boardship and in the colony, the Protector will submit for the information of Government the under-noted periodical reports and returns:

   (a) Monthly—A return showing the number and description of emigrants who have embarked for the colonies during the month immediately preceding that on which the return is due.

   (b) Annually—A report on the emigration of the preceding official year, giving particulars on any points of importance, and embracing detailed information . . . .

3. Fees under section 31 of the Indian Emigration Act must be levied on each emigrant as defined in section 3 of the Act.

4. In the event of any emigrant who is already registered for one colony desiring to emigrate to another, such emigrant may be re-registered for the colony elected. . . ; . . .

5   . . .

6.   . . .

Rules for the Guidance of the Medical Inspector of Emigrants

7.   . . .

8. The Medical Inspector shall exercise a careful supervision over the sanitary state of the emigration depots, and, when necessary, he should suggest to the Agent or officer in charge of the depot any alteration which, in a sanitary point of view, may seem to him likely to benefit the coolies; . . .

9. He is jointly responsible with the Protector of Emigrants for the eligibility, for emigration purposes, of vessels which take emigrants from this port, and is expected to be present with the Protector of Emigrants at the primary and final surveys of ships chartered for the conveyance of emigrants, of their ventilation, fittings, provisions, medical stores, and hospital arrangements. He shall also be present at the embarkation of emigrants, and shall see that everything is done to lessen the livelihood of disease and increase the comfort of the coolie.

10. No emigrant must be permitted to embark who is considered by the Medical Inspector to be physically unfit for the voyage, or who cannot do so without danger to his or her health or to that of others. . . .

Proceedings, General Department, Emigration Branch, December 1874

Form of Contract with Emigrants for British Guiana

No. 476 dated Calcutta, the 13th November 1874

From   H.A. Firth, Esq., Emigration Agent for British Guiana
To   J.G.G. Grant, Esq., Protector of Emigrants

In reply to your No. 1304 of 24th September last; I have the honour to enclose draft of a contract, which after your approval, I propose to have printed on the back of each registration certificate.

Contract made between the Emigration Agent for British Guiana at Calcutta, and the emigrant described on the other side of this sheet.

Such emigrant having engaged to proceed to British Guiana it is hereby agreed between said Emigration Agent and the emigrant as follows:

I. The emigrant shall be provided with a free passage to British Guiana in accordance with the existing Indian Emigration Act and Rules.

II. The emigrant, on arrival at British Guiana, shall be indentured to an employer by the Immigration Agent-General, under the orders of the Governor, to work on a plantation in the cultivation of the soil or the manufacture of the produce on every day, Sundays and holidays excepted, during five years, for seven hours in the Field, or ten hours in the factory.

III. The emigrant, if an able-bodied adult male of and above 15 years of age, shall be paid eight annas for each day's work; and if an adult male not able-bodied, or a minor male of and above 10 years and under 15 years, or a female adult or minor of and above 10 years shall be paid five annas four pie for each day's work; and all emigrants shall be paid in proportion for every extra hour of work. And if the emigrants elects to work by task instead of by time, the same wage shall be paid as is paid to un indentured labourers on the same or neighbouring plantation; which wage may be more—but never less than the minimum wage for day work. So soon as the emigrant shall have earned Rs.758, by day or task work, the indenture of that emigrant shall absolutely cease, notwithstanding the term of five years being unexpired. Infant emigrants under 10 years of age shall not be compelled to work; but should work be undertaken, the wage shall be in proportion to the capacity for work.

IV. Wages shall be paid weekly, in money, subject to no deductions, except for rations.

V. Suitable dwellings shall be provided for the emigrants at all times; and medical attendance, comforts, diet, medicine and hospital accommodation when sick, free of cost.

VI. The emigrant, after a continuous residence in British Guiana of ten years, shall be provided with a free passage back to Calcutta.

Proceedings, General Department, Emigration Branch, June 1877

Draft Rules amending Rules 23 and 29 of the rules relating to Emigration from the Port of Calcutta under Act VII of 1871

The following rules have been made by the Governor-General in Council under the powers conveyed by section 56 of Act VII of 1871 (The Indian Emigration Act), are applicable to emigration from the port of Calcutta.

23. The proportion of female emigrants to be embarked on each ship during the months of August to October both inclusive, shall be as nearly as practicable 25 adults females to every 100 adult males.

23A.   During the period from 1st November to the close of each season, the proportion shall be such number between 40 and 80 adult females to every 100 adult males at the Protection of Emigrants may fix for each ship.

23B.   If in any season the average fall below this, the Protector of Emigrants shall in exercising the discretion given him by the first clause of Rule 23A, so fix the proportion for the several ships dispatched during the period commencing with 1st November of the following season to its close, as to bring up the average proportion for the two seasons, if practicable to not less than 40 adult females to every 100 adult males.

(only relevant points have been cited)

Proceedings, General Department, Emigration Branch, November 1880

Annual Report

In regard to those of British Guiana Mr Firth intimated in July 1879 that in accordance with the existing diet scale sanctioned by the Government of Demerara, he had amended article V (Scale of ration) of the terms of agreement on which Indian emigrants where to be engaged for that colony. In submitting the revised scale for the approval of Government, it was observed that it did not appear to possess any decided advantage over the former one, except that it provided flour, which is likely to be preferred by the majority of emigrants, who are flour-eaters. Formerly 12 chittack of rice and 2 chittacks of dal were allowed to each adult. The rice has been reduced to 4 chittacks, and the dal $1^1/_2$ chittack, the reduction being apparently counter balanced by the substitution of one seer yams, plantain, sweet potatoes, lannias, cassava or cornmeal, or half a seer of flour. It was noticed that salt had been altogether omitted and looking to the importance of the article, the Government of India has desired to be informed of the reason for the omission, but the reply from the colony to the enquiry made on this question through Mr. Firth has not yet been received, though it is expected shortly.

TABLE 2.2: The Terms Offered to Intending Emigrants to the Four Sugar Colonies under British Possession since the 1871

Colony	Classification of emigrants	Work		Period of indenture	Wages, minimum rate claimable	Ration prescribed scale	Period of supply	Dwelling house	Medical cure & maintenance during sickness	Free return passage when claimable
		Nature	Duration							
1	2	3	4	5	6	7	8	9	10	11
British Guiana	Adult males from 15 and upwards males from 10 to 15 & females above 10 years of age	Cultivation of the soil, and manufacture of the produce	Six days in a week, holidays excepted and seven hours in the fields or ten hours in the buildings in each day	Five years	Daily Rs A P 24 cents 0 8 0 16 cents 0 8 0	For adult of above 15 years of age at a cost of 2 annas and 8 pics daily Rice—1½ lb 4 chittacks 0 kanchas Dal—4OZ 1½ chittacks 0 kanchas Coconut oil—1Z 0½ ch. 0 Kan or ghee Masala—¾ Z0 Ch 1½ Kan Masala—¾ Z0 Ch 1½ Kan Sugar—2Z, 1 Ch, 0 Kan Salt—½ Z For minors of and above 10, and under 15 years of age, half the above quantities at half the cost. For infants under 10 years of age ⅓ of the above quantities free of cost	From the first date of delivery to any employer until the first day of Oct then next following	Free of charge	Free of charge	After ten years continuous residence in the colony, five years having been passed under indenture

(Contd.)

Table 2.2 (contd.)

1	2	3	4	5	6	7	8	9	10	11
Trinidad	Adult males and females from 10/15 years and upwards	Cultivation of the soil, and manufacture of the produce	Six days in the week holidays excepted, and nine hrs each day	Five years	Daily 1SO ½ d = 0 8 4 Payable fortnightly	For adults from 10 years & upwards (daily) Rice—1 lb Dal—4OZ Ghee or—1Z Coconut oil Sugar—2Z For non-adult from 5–10 years half the above scale—Free of Charge	For two years at a cost of 2 annas and 8 pie per ration (for the year 1878–1885). First year under indenture (for the year 1886–1889)	Free of charge	Free of charge	After ten years continuous residence in the colony, five years having been passed under indenture
Jamaica	Adult males from 10 yrs & upwards Males from 12–16 years & females of any page	Cultivation of the soil, and manufacture of the produce	Six days in a week, holidays excepted, and seven hours in the fields or ten hours in the buildings in each day	Five years	Daily 1S = 0 8 0 9d = 0 6 0 Payable monthly	For adults: Daily Rice—1½ lb or Corn meal—2 lb Cooker cassava —2 lb Raw cassava—4 lb Raw yarns or cocoas—5 lb Monthly	For the first three months, or if necessary for the whole period of indenture at maximum	Free of charge	Free of charge	After ten

(Contd.)

Table 2.2 (*contd.*)

1	2	3	4	5	6	7	8	9	10	11
						Split peas—8 lb Salt fish—6 lb or mutton beef —8 lb or goat flesh—8 lb or sweet—1 pint or coconut oil Salt—1 lb Dry pepper—20 Z or pimento fuel sufficient	cost of 35.6 d weekly			Not provided by the colony
Mauritius	Males— Adult about 18 yrs Adult 15— 18 yrs Adult 12—	Cultivation of the soil, and manufacture of the produce and	Six days in a week, holidays excepted and seven hours in	Five years	Monthly: Rs. A. P. 10S = 5 0 0 8S = 4 0 0 6S = 3 0 0 5S = 2 8 0	For adults above 12 yrs weekly: Rice—1½ lb Pounded Maize—2 lb Cooked Monioc—2½ lb Raw ditto—5 lb	For whole period of indenture	Free of charge	Free of charge	
	15 yrs Minor above 10— 12 yrs Females— Adults male return emigrants Above 18 yrs— Above 14— 18 yrs	Domestic Services	the fields or ten hours in the buildings in each day		Daily: 6d 0 4 0 and a ration or rice payable Monthly: 6S = 3 0 0 11S = 5 0 0 9S = 4 8 0 Payable monthly	Monthly: Dal—80 Z Salt fish—8 Z Ghee or oil—4 Z Saltl—4 Z For non-adults and 12 years three-fourth of the above sale— free of charge.				

Source: Computed from Proceedings General Department Annual Reports.

PART II

3

Extent of Emigration

Causes and Decline

AFTER THE ABOLITION of slave trade in 1834, the demand for labour, particularly in the four sugar colonies, increased. Like the sugar colonies, India, too, was under British control, which enabled the former to import Indian labourers who worked for lower wages. Though this may have been one of the primary reasons behind emigration, there were other considerations too. In his report of 1883, Grierson stated that both India and China

are sub-tropical, their greater portion being outside the tropical belt. Here the conditions of life are very different. The climate is anything but equable, and is subject to sudden and extreme variations. . . . Here life is impossible without labour. . . . The inhabitants of India and China have, in the course of generations, developed into human beings possessing considerable agricultural skill and a wonderful capacity for continuous hard work.[1]

On the other hand, the socio-economic conditions in some parts of India also favoured the British Planters—they could get cheap labour on easy terms. This was the primary reason for labour absorption from India or, more precisely, through the Calcutta Port to the sugar colonies, mainly during the second half of the nineteenth century.

Material Conditions of the Origin

People from Bihar and the North-Western Provinces (NWP) comprised a large portion of labour migrating to the sugar colonies. Economic conditions in these areas were poor, which explains why so many emigrated. This view was supported by the Annual Report where Dr J.G. Garow Grant, Protector of Emigrants said, 'It seems probable that the absence of those causes such as dearness of food, scantiness of harvest and the like—which compel labourers to emigrate. . . .'[2] The situation has been analysed in the following paragraphs.

The people of Bihar suffered great economic hardship. Particular districts—Muzaffarpur, Sarun, Darbhanga, Monghyr, Bhagalpore, Patna, Gaya and Shahabad—emerged as major emigration districts within Bihar. In 1875, Sir Stewart Bayley, the Commissioner of the Patna Division said, 'Behar is a very poor country, and the material condition of the people very low. . . . The labourer's wage gives him subsistence, but only by adding earnings of his wife and family. Indebtedness is very general. . . .'[3]

The collector of Patna wrote about the ryots holding less than two and a half acres as '[t]hey can only take one full meal instead of two. They are badly housed and in the cold weather insufficiently clothed'. He also noted, 'Ordinarily, male labourers do not find employment for more than eight months of the year.'[4] In Darbhanga district, the collector said, '[T]here is no doubt that the bulk of the cultivating population are occupiers of small holdings. . . .'[5]

The condition of Gaya district was the worst among the above-mentioned districts. According to the collector's statement, around 40 per cent of the population was insufficiently fed. Again, a large number of people migrated from Shahabad district. A greater part of these emigrants belonged to the labouring class with an appreciable number of traders.[6] The material condition of the people of Muzaffarpur was also very poor, mostly due to excessive pressure of population on land, which led to an excess supply of labour over demand resulting in lower labour wages.[7]

The population pressure on land was excessive in Bihar. In 1875, Sir Steuart Bayley wrote: 'Over the culturable area of the division, with the single exception of North Champaran . . . there is hardly any waste land, and the pressure of the population per square mile is excessive, ranging in cultivated tracts between 500 and 750 per square mile—a population too, almost wholly agricultural. . . .'[8]

In the North-Western Provinces (NWP), the emigration took place mainly from its eastern districts. Agriculture was the main occupation in this region, which saw very small industrial development. But the agricultural condition was harsh and the methods used very primitive. In Ballia district, 'improvement in implements, system, and seed are practically unknown. The cultivator remains satisfied with his primitive plough, his simple means of fertilizing the soil, the traditional rotation of crops, and he pays no attention to the selection of seed'.[9] The agricultural condition of Gorakhpur district was still harsh. Cultivation was limited to a single harvest in a year.[10]

From several sources and data, it is clear that a good number of labourers emigrated from some districts of Bengal Presidency than from other parts of India. Thus, after discussing this criteria, Grierson raised a question: 'Is Coolie emigration more popular in some districts than in others, and if so, why?'[11] He himself gave an answer to this question as under:

It will be seen that Patna and Shahabad are not only great registering districts, but also great emigrating districts. Saran and Gaya, however, in which the registrations per million were small, have leaped to the front as birth districts of emigrants. Briefly we may say that the emigrating instinct is strong in Shahabad, Patna and Saran, and moderately strong in Gaya, and that it hardly exists elsewhere in the Presidency. . . . In every way emigration is most popular in Patna and Shahabad. It is also popular to a lesser extent in Saran. . . . The reason of this popularity is easy to see, and I have mentioned it several times—it is the fact of a large number of emigrants having returned who have given good accounts of the colonies.[12]

Changes in Recruiting Ground for Colonial Emigration

In the 1830s, primarily at the commencement of colonial emigration, the aboriginals of Chotonagpur Plateau, also known as 'hill coolies', were the main victims. The poor economic condition of such hill coolies and their expertise in such plantation jobs made them lucrative to the employers mainly through local recruiting agents. But in the 1850s, with the introduction of tea plantations in Assam, the hill coolies were gradually recruited for this purpose. They were mainly recruited for their physical strength needed for cutting forests and clearing the jungle lands.

In the later years, it has been seen that the demand for labour, especially from Bihar, in the tea gardens of Assam countered colonial emigration. Grierson in his report of 1883, mentioned an extract of Dr. V. Richard, the Protector of Emigrants, which says:

Colonial emigration from Bihar is much less important than that from the North-Western Provinces, and that it is doubtful whether it is advisable to force it on in Bihar too much. Bihar is the natural recruiting ground for Assam, and the supply for Assam is by no means equal to the demand, and it would be advisable to take any direct measures which would tend to diminish that supply.

'There is no colonial emigration from Chutia Nagpur, the natives of that tract preferring to go to Assam, and not being physically able to bear the long sea voyages to the colonies.'[13] Therefore, the main recruiting ground for sugar colonies was gradually extended to the NWP, since the people of Chotonagpur as well as some part of Bihar went for tea plantation in Assam. In support, the Annual report of the General Department, 1881 mentions as:

> It is obvious that the N-W-Provinces, as a source of supply, has been to the colonies what Chota Nagpur has been to the tea districts; while Behar has afforded common ground for colonial and inland recruiters. It is necessary to observe, however, that the collection of labourers for the colonies has apparently been confined more or less to the North Western parts of Behar, whereas the collection of labourers for the tea districts appears to have been more or less confined to the south-eastern parts of that division.[14]

Features of Emigrants
Place of Origin

In 1872–3, nearly three-fourths of the emigrants to the four sugar colonies were drawn from certain districts of the NWP, Oudh and central India (Table 3.1). One-fifth came from Bihar, while the contribution of Bengal was only 5 per cent. A very small percentage was collected from other parts of India.

A large proportion of immigrants to Mauritius came from certain district of Bihar for the years 1851 and 1854–5 as shown in Table 3.2. Table 3.3 shows that larger proportion of emigrants came from Bihar and the NWP and Oudh to four sugar colonies from 1875–6 to 1898–9. Table 3.4 shows the number of emigrants from several districts of Bengal, Bihar, NWP and Oudh to the four sugar colonies during the years 1870–1 and 1893. An increase in number of emigrants between these two years has been observed from some districts of NWP particularly to Demerara.

According to data from the Mauritius Archives on the purchase of land by Indian immigrants in different estates of Mauritius (Table 4.2), the vast majority of those immigrants came from different districts of Bihar, namely, Arrah, Gaya, Chuprah, Bhagalpore, Muzaffarpur, Ranchi, Hazaribagh, Monghyr and Patna. The districts of present-day eastern Uttar Pradesh, namely, Benares, Ghazipur and Azamgarh, were also important in this respect. Immigrants from Burdwan, Midnapore and Purulia districts of West Bengal also purchased land in certain estates of Mauritius.[15]

According to a report based on a sample survey for the period 1865–1917 conducted by sociologist Raymond T. Smith in British Guiana in 1958, and referring to data extracted from the archives of the Immigration

TABLE 3.1: Statement showing Number of Emigrants to
Mauritius, Demerara, Trinidad and Jamaica through Calcutta Port
from Some Selected Provinces during 1872–3

Province	Districts	Number of souls recruited for the colonies				
		Mauritius	Demerara	Trinidad	Jamaica	Total
North–Western Provinces, Oudh and Central India	Allahabad, Azimghur, Mirzapore, Benares, Ghazeepore, Goruckpore, Meerut, Cawnpore, Bareilly, Agra, Jhansie, Jounpore, Oudh, Lucknow, Seetapore, Sultanpore, Faizabad, Roy Bariely, Indore, Nagpore, Jubbulpore, Raepore, Remah, Rewah, Gwalior	2,255	4,801	3,726	1,481	12,263 (73.16)
Behar	Patna, Gaya, Arrah, Sarun, Tirhoot, Chumparun, Moonghyr, Bhaugulpore	2,263	964	77	56	3,360 (20.05)
Bengal	Calcutta, 24 Parganas, Howrah, Nuddea, Burdwan, Moorsheda–bad, Jessore, Pabna, Rangpore, Cooch Behar, Purneah, Chota Nagpore, Bancoorah, Beerbhoom, Midnapore, Santhal Pergunnahs, Dacca, Mymensing, Backer–gunge, Furreedpore	607	261	24	9	901 (5.38)
Others	—	137	61	23	16	237 (1.41)

Protector's Office
Fort William   J.G.G. Grant
The 18th June, 1873   Protector of Emigrants

Source: Proceedings, General Department, September 1873, Emigration Branch, p. 6.
Note: Bracket shows percentage.

Agent General's Office, Georgetown, British Guiana, most of the emigrants sailed from Calcutta port while a small number of ships sailed from Madras. A large proportion of emigrants, the survey showed, were from Bihar and the United Provinces of Agra and Oudh, which also established the fact that most of them embarked through the Calcutta port.

TABLE 3.2: District–wise Distribution of Emigrants to
Mauritius during the Years 1851 and 1854–5

Province/Districts	Number of emigrants to Mauritius	
	1851	1854–5
Bengal		
Bancoorah	323	143
Burdwan	84	41
Calcutta	30	12
24 Parganas	112	43
Other districts	141	94
TOTAL	**690**	**333**
	(9.93)	(4.00)
Bihar		
Shahabad	1,131	2,093
Sarun	319	348
Hazareebagh	303	393
Patna	457	434
Ranchi	286	292
Gaya	1,075	1,259
Other districts	557	685
TOTAL	**4,128**	**5,504**
	(59.41)	(66.11)
N–W–Ps and Oudh		
Azimghur	195	470
Benares	180	262
Ghazeepore	495	302
Goruckpore	102	122
Jounpore	128	169
Lucknow	137	125
Other districts	67	134
TOTAL	**1,304**	**1,584**
	(18.77)	(19.02)
Other Provinces	**826**	**905**
	(11.89)	(10.87)
GRAND TOTAL	**6,948**	**8,326**
	(100.00)	(100.00)

Source: General Department, 3 June 1852, No. 21 and General Department, 9 August 1855, No. 27.

Note: Bracket shows percentage.

From this sample study, it can be shown that 85.6 per cent emigrants to the sugar colonies of British Guiana were from several districts of Bihar and the United Provinces of Agra and Oudh. The study also shows that the most outmigrating region was the eastern districts of United Provinces.

TABLE 3.3: Proportion of Emigrants from Bihar, NWP and Oudh
to Four Sugar Colonies during 1875–6 to 1899–1900

Year	Proportion							
	Demerara		Trinidad		Jamaica		Mauritius	
	Bihar	NWP & Oudh	Bihar	NWP & Oudh	Bihar	NWP & Oudh	Bihar	NWP & Oudh
1875—6	29.00	68.28	17.00	74.11	12.00	84.09	32.34	57.78
1876–7	–	–	–	–	–	–	–	–
1877–8	8.15	80.83	13.85	73.41	–	–	38.33	56.12
1878–9	9.80	88.00	11.13	86.36	3.64	94.55	40.82	55.08
1879–80	13.00	74.42	18.10	75.80	12.57	83.33	45.46	45.46
1880–1	11.50	77.00	9.55	85.52	1.56	88.50	43.83	39.57
1881–2	10.76	74.27	37.00	81.47	–	–	–	–
1882–3	20.00	59.58	5.00	85.84	2.26	79.90	40.64	81.42
1883–4	23.44	65.00	17.32	64.26	–	–	38.61	44.15
1884–5	36.19	47.81	46.87	42.45	47.75	45.92	40.32	33.38
1885–6	43.30	48.92	51.87	43.24	–	–	–	–
1886–7	33.11	58.42	32.85	60.00	–	–	–	–
1887–8	22.68	73.44	20.75	74.27	–	–	–	–
1888–9	26.00	71.19	27.36	68.28	–	–	–	–
1889–90	18.71	78.52	28.00	68.28	–	–	43.00	52.25
1890–1	–	–	–	–	–	–	–	–
1891–2	–	–	–	–	–	–	–	–
1892–3	–	–	–	–	–	–	–	–
1893–4	15.90	77.90	24.00	68.54	38.06	50.62	25.13	68.92
1894–5	12.00	83.50	20.35	76.90	17.72	80.17	20.16	71.61
1895–6	8.24	90.00	4.60	94.35	5.11	93.19	6.65	92.07
1896–7	6.00	92.39	9.73	88.70	–	–	5.54	91.78
1897–8	11.00	87.60	9.30	86.33	–	–	–	98.00
1898–9	8.91	86.43	6.07	90.14	–	–	–	–
1899–1900	–	–	–	–	–	–	–	–

Source: Computed from Proceedings, General Department, Annual Reports, 1875–6 to 1898–9.

People of these districts were generally a mobile, landless labouring class that lived in poor, densely populated rural areas. According to Smith, 'The districts in the United Provinces and Bihar supplying the largest numbers in the sample were Basti (820), Azamgarh (585), Ghazeepore (544), Gonda (478), Fyzabad (386), Allahabad (294), Gorakhpur (291), Jaunpur (260), Shahabad (230), Lucknow (216).'[16]

Therefore, Smith's sample study corroborates the same fact found in the various primary sources of the Government of India—that a large

TABLE 3.4: Statement showing Number of Emigrants to
Demerara, Trinidad, Jamaica and Mauritius from Some Selected
Districts of Bengal, Bihar, NWP and Oudh through Calcutta Port
during 1870–1 and 1893

Province/District	Colonies importing Indian labour							
	Demerara		Trinidad		Jamaica		Mauritius	
	1870–1	1893	1870–1	1893	1870–1	1893	1870–1	1893
Bengal								
Calcutta	2	56	–	21	6	16	6	1
Burdwan	11	284	3	241	6	–	9	–
24 Parganas	7	623	4	483	5	–	9	–
Bihar								
Gya	179	N.A.	84	N.A.	78	N.A.	268	N.A.
Monghyr	76	53	2	–	14	–	18	–
Patna	200	423	40	112	86	48	140	–
Shahabad	346	343	208	358	125	61	543	108
Saran	136	103	39	41	74	7	75	–
N–W–Provinces								
Allahabad	193	530	227	130	204	–	22	107
Azamgarh	94	107	187	32	38	–	67	–
Benares	70	655	161	406	29	–	73	48
Cawnpore	42	1158	12	83	22	62	3	27
Ghazipore	212	291	259	199	122	–	214	38
Gorakhpur	72	489	62	48	46	41	32	–
Jounpur	67	139	36	180	46	–	18	–
Oudh								
Fyzabad	110	546	77	207	22	137	6	68
Gonda	N.A.	324	N.A.	17	N.A.	10	N.A.	4
Lucknow	653	530	139	–	85	–	29	–

Source: Computed from Proceedings, General Department, 1870–1, 1893.

proportion of emigrants came from present Uttar Pradesh, mostly from
its eastern districts, and also from Bihar (Table 3.5).

Age Distribution

One interesting observation is that a large proportion of emigrants to
the sugar colonies fall in the age group of 20–30 years as shown in
Table 3.6. This implies that the preference of the recruiters were young
people who could perform hard, strenuous jobs in those colonies.
Smith's sociological study in 1959 also observed that more than half,
i.e. 54 per cent, of the emigrants belonged to this age group, indicating
the fact that young people, particularly males, were sent to seek work
(Table 3.7).

TABLE 3.5: Places of Birth of a Sample of Emigrants from
India to British Guiana, 1865–1917

Province of birth	Number	Per cent
United Provinces	6,605	70.3
Bihar	1,440	15.3
Orissa	57	0.6
Bengal	131	1.4
Other Provinces	1,160	12.4
TOTAL	9,393	100.0

Source: Computed from Smith, 1959

TABLE 3.6: Proportion of Emigrants within the Age Group 20–30 years
to the Four Sugar Colonies during 1875–6 to 1899–1900

Year	Proportion of emigrants (20–30 years) to total emigrants			
	Demerara	Trinidad	Jamaica	Mauritius
1875–6	62.22	53.60	56.19	53.18
1876–7	–	–	–	–
1877–8	54.56	52.77	53.46	37.76
1878–9	66.06	62.39	54.55	34.43
1879–80	61.65	59.63	58.47	37.85
1880–1	60.44	59.96	63.35	43.40
1881–2	61.65	58.90	–	–
1882–3	61.64	58.94	59.55	53.12
1883–4	60.75	59.90	–	52.29
1884–5	58.26	52.94	58.07	52.08
1885–6	61.88	60.02	–	–
1886–7	51.73	55.61	–	–
1887–8	56.73	54.00	–	–
1888–9	60.11	63.83	–	–
1889–90	63.54	56.61	–	56.20
1890–1	–	–	–	–
1891–2	–	–	–	–
1892–3	–	–	–	–
1893–4	72.05	69.26	76.75	69.95
1894–5	69.75	64.14	69.76	79.01
1895–6	72.06	70.74	79.75	74.75
1896–7	71.20	71.57	–	81.07
1897–8	82.34	82.50	–	78.88
1898–9	76.26	79.26	–	–
1899–1900	–	–	–	–

Source: Computed from Proceedings, General Department Annual Report 1875–6 to
1898–9.

TABLE 3.7: Age and Sex of Immigrants from India to British Guiana
during the period 1865–1917

Age Group	Percentages to total number of emigrants to British Guiana		
	Males	Females	Total
Under 2	1.3	1.3	2.6
2–10	5.0	3.8	8.8
11–20	21.7	8.1	29.8
21–30	38.2	15.8	54.0
31–40	3.5	0.9	4.4
Over 40	0.2	0.2	0.4
TOTAL	69.9	30.1	100.0

Source: Smith, 1959

Sex Ratio

Until 1870, with some exceptions, the sex ratio among emigrants was very low (Appendix III-A). This fact indicates that initially single men, distressed by their poor economic conditions, went to such long distances looking for a job, leaving their families behind.

From 1877 onwards (up to 1899), the sex ratio increased, in comparison to the previous decades (Appendices III-A and III-B). This increase was mainly due to the statutory law of maintaining the proportion to not less than 40 women to every 100 men for each shipment. This rule was restored during the 1880s by establishing some administrative measures. According to Smith, the sex ratio of emigrants to British Guiana was about 430, which shows that there were about 70 males to 30 females among the emigrant population (Table 3.7).

Caste and Religion

Though it is clear from various evidences that the majority of people emigrating to sugar colonies were from the lower castes, members of the higher castes also formed a considerable portion (Appendix X). Usually, the lack of an alternative to occupations other than agriculture, coupled with overcrowding in farming, presumably, is the primary reason for emigration among higher caste people. Smith, in his survey, showed that a large proportion of the emigrants belonged to the lower caste—mainly agricultural and other labouring castes—whereas most of them were Hindus (see Table 3.8). The overall view of this survey has a common link with the data procured from various sources of Government of India.

TABLE 3.8: Religion and Caste of a Sample of Emigrant from
Calcutta to British Guiana, 1865–1917

Group	Number	Per cent
Brahmin and Allied Castes	191	2.1
Kshatriya and Allied Castes	865	9.6
Kayastha	31	0.3
Baniya	39	0.4
Cultivator Castes	1,492	16.6
Grazier Castes	1,215	13.5
Artisan Castes	778	8.7
Petty Trader and Confectioner Castes	104	1.2
Fisherman and Boatmen Castes	508	5.7
Menial and Labouring Castes	2,032	22.6
Miscellaneous Hindu Castes	252	2.8
TOTAL HINDU	7,507	83.6
Muslims	1,465	16.3
Christians	7	0.1
TOTAL	8,979	100.0

Source: Smith, 1959

Fluctuation in Labour Emigration:
Its Various Reasons

Recruitment to sugar colonies varied from year to year for various reasons. As has been stated earlier, one of the important reasons was the increasing demand for labour in the tea gardens in Assam, especially from Bihar, one of the key recruiting zones. In 1883, Grierson reported:

Recruitment not so good this year, as the Kachar tea-planters are vigorously opening out new recruitment grounds in Bihar. These recruiters almost monopolized the business at times, for not only is the distance less, but the recruits get wages two months in advance—a hint which might be taken up by the Colonial Emigration Agent.[17]

The number of indigenous emigrants from Bihar and Bengal were comparatively higher than those from the NWP and Oudh in 1885. In the Annual Report on Colonial Emigration for the last nine months of the year 1885, the Protector of Emigrants stated:

It appears that during the months in which the largest number of coolies were being collected for the colonies, the grain market for the NWP and Oudh were on the whole well supplied; whereas those of Bengal and Behar were suffering from scarcity that resulted in dearness of food grains, and of rice especially. The absence during the hot season of sufficient rain, followed in September and October by inundations affecting parts of Behar and the Burdwan and Presidency Divisions, had proved sufficiently injurious to the crops to maintain, during the period of active requirement, the high prices that favoured emigration from the Lower Provinces. . . .[18]

The fall in labour demand in 1885 is another example of the fluctuating nature of labour emigration—to several sugar colonies through Calcutta Port. In a resolution of the Annual Report on Colonial Emigration in 1886, it was stated: 'The year was marked by a striking falling off in the demand for Indian labourers. The falling off is not explained in the protector's report, but is understood to be due to the declining state of the sugar industry, in which the emigrants are mainly employed.'[19]

In the mid-1880s, the increasing production and export of beet sugar had an effect on the fortunes of the cane sugar producing industries (discussed earlier in Chapter 2). In a letter to the secretary to the Government of Bengal on 19 December 1889, Surgeon-Major D.W.D. Comins, Protector of Emigrants, Calcutta, wrote, 'I would here point out that the demand for labour in the colonies is almost entirely dependent on the fluctuations in the beetroot crop in Europe; and previously to the report of the Finance Committee, there had been in 1885 and 1886 a lessened demand for labour. From 1887, onwards however, the colonial sugar trade began to improve.'[20] It has been seen that in 1886 the total number of people registered for emigration to the sugar colonies was higher in the NWP and Oudh compared to those from Bihar and Bengal. In this context, Dr J.G. Garrow Grant says, 'if the two emigration seasons of 1884 and 1885 be excluded, it may be said that for years past natives of the NWPs and Oudh have responded in the largest numbers to the labour requisition of the colonies. . .'.[21]

Thus, fluctuation in the number of emigrants to sugar colonies was a result of variation in the crop (beetroot) production. However, in the decade 1890–1900, the planters felt that their demand for labour could be met by those Indian labourers settled earlier.

Industrial Development in Bengal and Inland Labour Demand

Industrialization in India started in the mid of the nineteenth century. With the inclusion of Calcutta as the British capital, several colonial enterprises were set up in Bengal, e.g. tea plantations, collieries, jute textile manufacturers, etc., which generated a demand for different kinds of industrial labour force. Jute spinning and weaving has been the chief manufacturing industry in Bengal, which concentrated mainly in the Calcutta metropolitan areas. Tea plantation in Darjeeling and Jalpaiguri districts comes net. Coal mining industry was concentrated in Asansol-Ranigung area of Burdwan district. This development accelerated with the introduction of Indian capital to the fields of cotton textile, rice milling, oil milling, sugar production, paper mills etc. Initially local labour mainly from the contiguous districts fulfilled this demand. But with the growth of industries labour became in short supply and a workforce was needed from outside Bengal. This demand for labour was large in Calcutta and other industrial districts of Bengal viz. Hooghly, Howrah, twenty-four parganas, and Burdwan. Thus a new direction of employment opportunity gradually opened up for the poor people of Bihar and North Western Provinces and interstate migration from these states to Bengal started by the last quarter of the nineteenth century.

Apart from colonial emigration and inland migration towards the tea districts of Assam due to the Industrial Revolution in the twentieth century in Bengal, a new direction of employment opportunities gradually opened up for the poor in Bihar and the NWP.

An idea of the incidence of this internal migration can be obtained from the census figures too. Reports of Bengal Census 1881 states that 46 per cent of the total immigrants to Bengal from Bihar came from its most emigrating districts namely Patna, Gaya, Muzaffarpur, Sarun and Shahabad districts. Tables 3.10 and 3.11 clearly indicate that the bulk of immigrants came from distance states and mostly attracted by the opportunities in Calcutta, twenty-four parganas and Howrah. Percentage of these immigrants rose by more than 10 per cent within a decade, i.e. in the year 1891 and 1901, nd this impact was more perceptible in Howrah and twenty-four parganas districts.

In 1878, the commissioner of Presidency Division reported, 'The large factories (in the 24 Parganas district) attract hands from Behar'.[22] Two years later, he also pointed out that 'natives of Behar and the North Western Provinces come to Barasat and Barrackpore for work in the factories in the sub-divisions. . .'.[23] There were jute and cotton mills in the Hooghly and Howrah districts where wages were very high.[24] These mills and factories attracted labourers from Bihar and the NWP (illustrated in Table 3.9).

In 1882, the police commissioner of Calcutta informed the Bengal government that 'at most jute factories, the employees are . . . principally composed of people from the Behar and other up country districts'.[25] Beginning from the last quarter of the nineteenth century, a large share of migrants came from some particular districts in Bihar, namely, Patna, Gaya, Shahabad, Saran, Muzaffarpur, Darbhanga and Monghyr. At the

TABLE 3.9: Percentage of Migrant Workers in Certain Mills,
Factories and Industrial Concerns in 24 Parganas, Howrah, and
Hooghly Districts of Bengal, 1897

Sl. No.	Name and locality of concerns	Percentage of up country migrant to total workers
	24 Parganas District	
1.	Gouripore Co. Ltd., Naihati	53.4
2.	Kankinarah Jute Mills	84.5
3.	Anglo Indian Jute Mills, Jagoddal	74.2
4.	Alliance Jute Mills, Jagoddal	56.4
5.	Dunbar Cotton Mills, Shamnagore	81.3
6.	Shamnagore Jute Factory	88.9
7.	Titagarh Paper Mills	73.4
8.	Khardah Jute Mills	53.5
9.	Kamarhati Jute Mills	73.9
10.	North Factory, Baranagar Jute Mills	71.0
11.	South Factory, Baranagar Jute Mills	61.1
12.	Titagurh Jute Mills	73.9
	Hooghly District	
1.	Champdany Jute Mills	61.8
2.	Indian Jute Mills, Serampore	37.5
3.	Victoria Jute Mills, Teliniparah	52.4
4.	Hastings Jute Mills, Serampore	65.5
	Howrah District	
1.	Bally Paper Mills, Bally	55.0
2.	Ghusery Cotton Mills, Ghusery	39.0
3.	Central Jute Mills, Ghusery	54.2
4.	Victoria Cotton Mills, Ghusery	26.2
5.	B.I.S.N. Co. Ltd. Iron Works, Salkea	40.5
6.	Burn & Co. Ltd., Howrah	36.7
7.	Sibpur Jute Mills, Sibpur	45.3
8.	Ganges Jute Mills, Sibpur	84.3
9.	Boureah Cotton Mills, Boureah	22.8
10.	Fort Gloster Jute Mills, Fort Gloster	34.3

Source: Computed from Proceeding, Judicial Department, Police Branch, September 1897, File P 3–p/21 1–9 & 11–15 Nos. 83–103, taken from Ghosh (2001).

same time, the districts of the eastern portion of the NWP were mainly responsible for the flow of migration towards Bengal. Those districts were mainly Ballia, Ghazipur, Jaunpur, Gorakhpur and Benares. The people migrated from these districts to the industrial districts of West Bengal.[26] The gradual increase in flow of migrants from Ghazipur district towards Bengal, or more precisely, towards Calcutta and Howrah, was due to the 'increased passenger traffic of the railways, and also in the remarkable amounts remitted to the district through the agency of the post office'.[27]

Although emigrants from Gorakhpur mainly concentrated in the districts of Calcutta and Howrah, 'the volume of such migration' was 'small in comparison with that from all parts of the Benares division, in which labour is more abundant and the pressure of the population on the land is far more severe'.[28] The emigrants of 'Benares had left their homes to

TABLE 3.10: Immigrants to the Industrial Districts of Bengal from Outside Bengal, 1891

(in %)

Sl. No.	Immigrants from	Burdwan	Hooghly	Howrah	24 parganas	Total of four districts
1	Contiguous Districts	74.13	79.14	50.19	26.63	53.48
	Other Districts of					
2	Bengal Proper	4.39	4.77	7.81	20.47	10.73
3	Outside Bengal	18.62	12.27	36.14	39.47	28.43
4	Orissa	0.52	2.75	3.80	9.63	4.85
5	Elsewhere	2.34	1.07	2.06	3.80	2.51
	TOTAL	100.00	100.00	100.00	100.00	100.00

Source: Computed from Census of Lower provinces of Bengal, 1891. Provincial Table III.

Note: Outside Bengal includes Bihar, N-W-P and Chota Nagpur. N-W-P renamed in 1901 as United Provinces and now Uttar Pradesh.N-W-P includes the region from Benares to Punjab, including Oudh. Orissa has not been included within the category of outside Bengal, since this state have no impact on colonial emigration in our study.

TABLE 3.11: Immigrants to the Industrial Districts of Bengal from Outside Bengal, 1901

Sl. No.	Immigrants from	Burdwan	Hooghli	Howrah	24 parganas	Calcutta	Total of five districts
1	Contiguous Districts	68.33	65.84	34.20	29.41	17.13	33.58
	Other Districts of						
2	Bengal Proper	3.93	1.97	3.33	10.95	28.76	16.22
3	Outside Bengal	21.40	25.86	50.23	45.96	40.64	38.58
4	Orissa				5.31	8.65	4.75	4.38
5	Elsewhere	6.34	6.33	6.93	5.03	8.72	7.25
	TOTAL	100.00	100.00	100.00	100.00	100.00	100.00

Source: Computed from Census of India, 1901, vol. VI, Appendix I, Migration Statement, taken from Dhar (2001).

Note: Outside Bengal includes Bihar, N-W-P and Chota Nagpur. N-W-P renamed in 1901 as United Provinces and now Uttar Pradesh. N-W-P includes the region from Benares to Punjab, including Oudh. Orissa has not been included within the category of outside Bengal, since this state have no impact on colonial emigration in our study.

obtain work in the coal fields of Bengal. . .'.[29] A large number of migrant labourers of Ghazipur and Ballia districts had to 'resort to the industrial centres of Howrah, Calcutta, and elsewhere. . .'.[30] Outmigrants of the NWP also sought work in the Raniganj coal mines of Burdwan and factories of Hooghly district.[31]

A study of changes in the occupational structure of the working population in Bengal since the beginning of the twentieth century also reveals that most of the industrial workers are immigrants from UP, Bihar, the Central Provinces, Orissa and Madras, while in the plantation areas of Jalpaiguri and Darjeeling districts of Bengal, a large number of workers migrated from Chotonagpur Plateau, Nepal and Central Provinces.[32]

From earlier paragraphs, it becomes clear that composition of population for colonial emigration and inland out-migration towards industrial districts of Bengal was almost same. So it may be summed up that due to the enhancement of communication in India an also to the industrial resurgence in Bengal, a new direction of migration have been opened up to Bengal from Bihar and NWP and supply of efficient emigrants to overseas turned down, which in due course resulted in the decline in colonial emigration, especially to the four sugar colonies.

Notes

1. George A. Grierson, 'Report on Colonial Emigration from the Bengal Presidency', General Department, Emigration Branch, Appendix A, File 15-20/21, Calcutta: West Bengal State Archives (hereafter WBSA), June 1883, p. 35.
2. Government of Bengal, General Department, Emigration Branch, November 1881, Proceedings, p. 31, Calcutta: WBSA.
3. W.W. Hunter, *A Statistical Account of Bengal*, vol. XVIII, London: Trubner & Co., 1877, pp. 34–5.
4. Government of Bengal, Revenue Department, *Report on the Condition of the Lower Classes of Population in Bengal*, Calcutta: Bengal Secretariat Press, 1888, p. 6.
5. Government of Bengal, Revenue Department, *Report on the Condition of the Lower Classes of Population in Bengal*, Calcutta: Bengal Secretariat Press, 1888, pp. 7–9.
6. Government of Bengal, District Census Report, Report on the Census of the District of Shahabad, 1891, pp. 53–4.
7. Government of Bengal, General Department, Miscellaneous Branch, Proceedings, Annual General Report, Patna Division, Calcutta: WBSA, November 1877.
8. Government of Bengal, Revenue Department, *Report on the Condition of the Lower Classes of Population in Bengal*, Calcutta: Bengal Secretariat Press, 1888, pp. 7–9.
9. H.R. Nevill, *Gazetteers of the United Provinces of Agra and Oudh, Ballia District*, vol. XXX, Allahabad: Superintendent of Government Press, 1907, p. 34.

10. H.R. Nevill, *Gazetteers of the United Provinces of Agra and Oudh, Gorakhpur District*, vol. XXXI, Allahabad: Superintendent of Government Press, 1909.

11. George A. Grierson, 'Report from Colonial Emigration from the Bengal Presidency', General Department, Emigration Branch, Appendix A, File 15-20/21, June 1883, Calcutta: WBSA, p. 41.

12. Ibid., pp. 42–3.

13. Ibid., Diary, p. 1.

14. Government of Bengal, General Department, Emigration Branch, Proceedings, Calcutta: WBSA, November 1881, p. 8.

15. Richard Blair Allen, 'Creoles, Indian Immigrants and the Restructuring of Society and Economy in Mauritius, 1767–1885', unpublished Ph.D. dissertation, University of Illinois, Michigan, 1983, p. 248.

16. Raymond T. Smith, 'Some Social Characteristics of Indian Immigrants to British Guiana', *Population Studies*, vol. 13, no. 1, 1959, pp. 34–9.

17. Grierson, 'Report from Colonial Emigration from the Bengal Presidency', Diary, pp. 8–9.

18. Government of Bengal, General Department, Emigration Branch, Proceedings, Calcutta: WBSA, December 1886, p. 7.

19. Government of Bengal, General Department, Emigration Branch 'Annual Report on Colonial Emigration', Resolution, Calcutta: WBSA, December 1886, p. 23.

20. Government of Bengal, General Department, Emigration Branch, Proceedings, Calcutta: WBSA, May 1890, p. 31.

21. Government of Bengal, General Department, Emigration Branch, Proceedings, 'The Report by the Protector of Emigrants to British and Foreign Colonies for the year 1886', Calcutta: WBSA, August 1887, File 15–18, p. 20.

22. Ranjit Dasgupta, 'Factory Labour in Eastern India: Sources of Supply, 1885–1946', *The Indian Economic and Social History Review*, vol. XIII, no. 3, July–September 1976, p. 287, quoted from Bengal, 'Divisional Commissioner's Annual Report for the Presidency Division for 1877–78', General Miscellaneous, nos. 5–6, September 1878, Calcutta: WBSA.

23. Dasgupta, 'Factory Labour in Eastern India', p. 287, quoted from Bengal, 'Divisional Commissioner's Annual Report for the Presidency Division for 1879–80', General Miscellaneous, nos. 8–10, August 1880, Calcutta: WBSA.

24. Government of Bengal, General Department, Miscellaneous Branch, Proceedings, Annual General Report, Burdwan Division, for 1879–80, File no. 38-33/34, 38-35, Calcutta: WBSA, September 1880.

25. Dasgupta, 'Factory Labour in Eastern India', p. 287, quoted from Home, Judicial, no. 220, National Archives of India, September 1883.

26. Chandralekha Ghosh, 'Migration in West Bengal during the Period 1872–1991: An Empirical Analysis', Unpublished Ph.D. dissertation, Kolkata: Jadavpur University, 2001.

27. H.R. Nevill, *Gazetteers of the United Provinces of Agra and Oudh, Gazipur District*, vol. XXI, Allahabad: Superintendent of Government Press, 1909, p. 79.

28. H.R. Nevill, *Gazetteers of the United Provinces of Agra and Oudh, Gorakhpur District*, vol. XXXI, Allahabad: Superintendent of Government Press, 1909, p. 92.

29. H.R. Nevill, *Gazetteers of the United Provinces of Agra and Oudh, Benares District*, vol. XXIV, Allahabad: Superintendent of Government Press, 1909, p. 86.

30. H.R. Nevill, *Gazetteers of the United Provinces of Agra and Oudh, Balia District*, vol. XXX, Allahabad: Superintendent of Government Press, 1907, p. 65.

31. Government of Bengal, General Department, Emigration Branch, Proceedings, Calcutta: WBSA, November 1891.

32. Sutapa Dhar, 'Changes in Occupational Structure and Economic Development of West Bengal, 1901–1991', Unpublished Ph.D. dissertation, Kolkata: Jadavpur University, 2001.

SUPPORTING DOCUMENTS

Proceedings, General Department, 13th October 1859, No. 3

Duties of the Emigration Agent in India for Jamaica

1. The Emigration agent will be instructed by the Governor what number of emigrants he is to provide from time to time.

2. He will thereupon take steps for endeavouring to collect the requisite number of eligible people to be at the Port of departure in the course of the appointed season for emigration. They must be sober, industrious, of general good character and have been in the habit of working in works of husbandry. They must be also in good health, free from all bodily or mental defects and must in all respects be capable of performing agricultural labour.

3. It is understood that the females shall form one-fourth of the whole number of the Emigrants, and that this proportion will be gradually increased, but upon this point the views and instructions of Her Majesty's government and of the Government of India from time to time must be rigidly attended to.

4. Single women of over 35 and single men over 40 years of age are ineligible.

5. Families in which there are more than two children under seven, or than three under ten years—widowers and widows with younger children cannot be accepted.

6. In the collection of Emigrants travelling and collecting Agents may be employed if necessary subject to approval of the authority of India, but the at most economy must be exercised in the employment of such agents as may be consists with the main subject of obtaining suitable agricultural Emigrants.

7. The Emigration Agent will take every means to prevent irregularities, deception, abuse or misrepresentation by the subordinate Agents in the collection of Emigrants and in bringing them from the interior.

8, Proper provision must be made for the lodging and maintenance at the depot of the people brought from a distance, while at the place of embarkation, and the opportunity should be taken while the people are there of dividing them into messes and accustoming them to the regularity, cleanliness and order which it is intended they should observe on board ship

[Only relevant points have been cited]

Proceedings, General Department, Emigration Branch, April 1867, Page 32

[No. 49]   From   Captain C. Burbank, Protector of Emigrants at Calcutta
           To   S.C.Bayley, Esq., Officiating Secretary to the Government of Bengal, No. 127, dated the 5th April, 1867

In obedience to the directions contained in your letter No. 1208 of the 9th ultimo, I have the honour to submit annual reports in duplicate for each colony to which emigrants were despatched from this port under Act XIII of 1864 for the year 1866-67 . . . the total number of emigrants (including women and children) dispatched during the period under review amounts in the aggregate to ten thousand one hundred and seventy five, which is a considerable decrease when compared with the operations of last year, viz.

1865–66	19,963
1866–67	10,175

In the margin is briefly noted the names of the Colonies and the number of emigrants imported by each respectively.

Mauritius	478
British Guiana	4,509
Trinidad	2,993
Jamaica	1,705
St. Vincent	490
	10,175

These figures denote that emigration to Mauritius has fallen off very considerably during the past year chiefly from two causes: firstly, owing to the high price of grain imported for the consumption of labourers in the Colony; and secondly, from the depressed state of the agricultural prospects of the Island, in consequence of the recent severe drought, the effects of which are likely to be disastrous. For these reasons emigration on account of Government is temporarily suspended. There are, however, a number of old emigrants returning to Mauritius at their own expense, paying their passage—a fact which speaks for itself, as indicative of the general condition and prospects of labourers in that country.

Proceedings, General Department, March 1875, File 21–12

Pressure of Population in parts of Bengal, and its Alleviation

1. The Lieutenant-Governor has directed me to note any impressions I may have gained, or opinions I may have formed, on the subject of the pressure of population in Bengal, and on the question how emigration can best be promoted from any tracts where the pressure may now be excessive. During the last two months I have visited all the distressed districts; I travelled by day as much as I could. The country was covered with splendid crops; the winter rice was being cut,

and the spring crops were above ground. So far as I had opportunity, I discussed points bearing on the important question now under notice with natives and with European officers.

2. I should mention that I have seen the remarks on the present subject recorded in the Lieutenant-Governor's famine Minute of the 31st October. What is there well said need not be repeated by me. I will only offer such additional or confirmatory observations as occur to me.

3. In the first place no district I visited, except Sarun, seemed to be cultivated to the last acre, or nearly to the last acre. Parts of Tirhoot, of Shahabad, and of Patna, seemed to be cultivated as fully as possible, but then the other parts there seemed to be considerable areas still available for cultivation. Even in Sarun and best-tilled parts of Tirhoot and Shahabad, the area of irrigated land is very small indeed. If water could be made available to these tracts in considerable quantity, the land would of course employ more labour and would yield a larger produce.

4. . . .

5. The only place where a large number of common labourers were employed during December was on the Sone Canal in Shahabad. Of these labourers a little more than half belonged to the Shahabad district, and somewhat less than half (speaking roughly) came from Ghazeepore and other districts of the North-Western Provinces. The engineers of the special divisions informed me that they were unable to hire labourers in any number until the middle or end of January, when the rice cutting was done. Rice cutting in Bengal is of course a longer and heavier business than the wheat harvest in England.

14 February 1975   C. BERNARD

Proceedings, General Department, November 1876

No. 1112A, dated Calcutta, the 31st October 1876.

From   Dr. J.G. Grant, Protector of Emigrants, Calcutta
To   The Officiating Secretary to the Government of Bengal, Political
            Department

. . . annual report on emigration from the port of Calcutta to the several British and foreign colonies during the official year 1875–76.

It will be seen that the number of emigrants admitted into the depots during the past year fell short of the number of the previous year by 12,267 souls, and therefore the extent of accommodation being about the same in each of the years under comparison, necessarily more than met the requirements of the season.

From the comparatively small number who were actually induced during the year to emigrate on the conditions offered, it would appear that when there is no famine or serious scarcity the present terms do not prove so attractive as to secure recruits in sufficient number to satisfy the requisitions of colonies making large demands for Indian labour. For example demand made by Demerara was not satisfied, and this although the rate of wages and other advantages offered appear sufficiently liberal. I am inclined, however, to the opinion that the provision of a free return passage after 10 years residence in the colony is not a very encouraging feature to the average coolie.

Emigrants are necessarily drawn from the poorest classes, and so unusual it is for such labourers in this country to earn more than a few annas daily, that it is difficult for many of them to believe that it will be possible for them to earn and save enough in about five years to pay for their return passages; while the prospects of having to remain ten years away from their homes before they can be entitled to a free return passage involves so many doubts, risks, and contingencies that many of them rather than venture so far abroad, prefer to bear the poverty and ills they know at home, and this all the more readily as their wants are few.

. . . The large deficiency on the supply of labour for Demerara may be ascribed to the comparative cheapness of food and probably in some degree at least to the inadequacy of the terms in respect of a free return passage to meet certain considerations which must seriously influence the Indian labour in determining as to whether he will emigrate—considerations such as the loss of caste; the separation for many years from home and friends; the chance of never returning; his utter ignorance of the colony offering employment and consequent inability to estimate satisfactorily the value or otherwise of the inducement held out to him. In addition to the above causes there were others which served to reduce considerably the total number of emigrants dispatched during the year under review as compared with that of the previous year.

Proceedings, General Department, Miscellaneous Branch, August 1880

Annual Report of the Presidency Division for the Year 1879–80

File 38–8/9 No. 24 RG, dated Alipore, the 29th June 1880

From   J. Monro, Esq., Officiating Commissioner of the Presidency Division.
To   The Secretary to the Government of Bengal, General Department

I have the honour to submit the Annual General Administration Report of the Presidency Division for 1879–80.

Emigration and Immigration

. . . A number of persons going to Assam, the West Indies, etc., pass through the 24 Pergunnahs district, and are registered at Alipore. During the year the names of 2,426 emigrants were registered. Of these, 664 went to Assam, Cachar and Sylghet, and 1,762 to Demerara, Trinidad, the Mauritius and other places.

Proceedings, General Department, Emigration Branch, December 1883

RESOLUTION (Pages 31–33)

The real and only serious obstacles to recruitment for the Colonies has, doubtless, been, and must continue to be, the objection of the people themselves to emigrate, due to caste prejudices, attachment to their homes, general ignorance of the conditions of life and prospects in the colonies, and unwillingness to leave their villages in seasons of prosperity and cheap food. The ignorance and prejudices of the people may, to a large extent, be removed, and towards this the Agencies themselves can contribute by the employment of return emigrants in recruitment, by helping to promote regular correspondence between the Colonies and this Country. . . .

. . . The large number of Brahmins would indicate that caste prejudice is, after all, not so strong an obstacle to emigration as is generally believed.

By order of the Lieut.-Governor of Bengal
A.P. Mac. Donnell, Officiating Secretary of the
Government of Bengal

4

Effects of Emigration

THE MOST IMPORTANT question related to emigration is this: What are the benefits and problems arising from large-scale emigration, with relation to the immigrating country as well as the country of origin? Although international cooperation between emigrant and immigrant countries could have helped maximize the benefits of emigration, in general, immigrating countries undertook labour emigration as a source of short-term economic benefit. They also treated emigrants as cheap labour and used them to meet skill shortages. On the other hand, among the emigrating countries doubts were expressed about the benefit of emigration, which could not be prevented in situations of severe population pressure. As a result, they tried to regulate movement to protect their citizens abroad.

The probable benefits and crises arising from Indian emigration to the four sugar colonies involves some micro-level effects on individual migrants, their families and communities and macro-level effects on both the countries of destination and the country of origin. This micro- and macro-level cost–benefit analysis is summarized in the following paragraphs.

Benefits from Emigration

The four sugar colonies undoubtedly benefitted from the importation of indentured coolies from India. For Mauritius, besides sustaining the prosperous plantation industry, a large influx of indentured labourers from India transformed the racial and ethnic composition of the colony. The report of the Government of Mauritius provided useful information on the ethnic composition of the country's population, which had changed enormously. The tendency for Mauritius planters was to rely more and more as years passed, on Indo-Mauritians, i.e. Indians born on the island, in order to reduce the cost of importation of labourers as well as to avail labour at a cheaper rate. The percentage of Indian population over the total resident population of Mauritius from 1846 to 1861 ranged from 35 to 55 per cent.[1] This trend was also observed in every British colony to which emigration from India had taken place over a long period.

The increase of these settled and unindentured population was beneficial to the sugar colonies and India. J.W.P. Muir-Mackenzie in his report on conditions of Indian immigrants in Mauritius has explained this importance of emigration and concluded that: 'The colonies on the one hand obtain to their hand a supply of labour sufficient for their needs. India, on the other hand, rids itself permanently, and to the distinct advantage of the emigrants, of a certain surplus of its population.'[2]

This advantage to India proved to be more effective especially in times of famine or distress. The economic circumstances of the famine-striven areas overwhelmingly favoured the emigration agents for collecting labourers at cheaper rates through Calcutta Port. Thus, famine was yet another notable factor pushing emigrants from districts in the north Indian plains and Bihar during the 1840s. This hypothesis finds confirmation in a despatch letter by Lord Salisbury to the Governor-General of India, dated 24 March 1875, that states:

Having regard to the greatness of our Indian population, and to the probability that, under the protection which the British Government affords from depopulation by war, and as far as possible, from famine and other evils, that population must continue very greatly to increase, especially in the healthier and more densely peopled parts of the country, where the numbers already press on the means of subsistence, and the lowest classes are at all times little removed from want, it appears to me that, from an Indian point of view, it is desirable to afford an outlet from these redundant regions into the tropical and sub-tropical dominions of Her Majesty, where people who hardly earn a decent subsistence in their own country may obtain more lucrative employment and better homes. While then, from an Indian point of view, emigration, properly regulated, and accompanied by sufficient assurance of profitable employment and fair treatment, seems a thing to be encouraged on grounds of humanity, with a view to promote the well-being of the poorer classes, we may also consider, from an imperial point of view, the great advantage which must result from peopling the warmer British possessions, which are rich in natural resources and only want population, by an intelligent and industrious race to whom the climate of these countries is well suited, and to whom the culture of the staples suited to the soil, and the modes of labour and settlement, are adapted. In this view also it seems proper to encourage emigration from India to Colonies well fitted for an Indian population. Under extraordinary circumstances, such as famine, flood, or other great calamities, when large numbers of the poorer classes are deprived of the means of subsistence, or are left without house and home, the Government officers might themselves engage emigrants for those Colonies which have agreed to receive people recruited under such circumstances.[3]

At the end of the indentured period, the Indian emigrants, primarily from the peasant class, wanted to own the lands and also retain their cultural identity. The Sanderson Committee reports:

The conditions of service for males in all the more distant Crown Colonies are a five years' indenture and five years subsequent residence in the Colony, after which the immigrant is entitled to a free or assisted passage. It is understood that after the first five years period of indentured service the immigrant is free to engage in any occupation open to the rest of the inhabitants, and is given facilities for settling in an independent position on the land.

To this latter condition we attach much importance. We agree with the view taken by Lord Salisbury in his despatch of March 1875, that it should be an indispensable condition of indentured emigration that Indians who have completed their term of indenture should be in all respects free men, subject to no Labour Ordinances and with personal privileges no where inferior to those of any other class of His Majesty's subjects resident in the Colony. The immigrants, on completion of their indenture, should be free either to return to India or to settle as free citizens in the colony. Drawn as they are from the agricultural labour classes, they usually, when they settle in the Colony, desire to become proprietors of agricultural land, and such a settlement of peasant proprietors is in the interests of the colony no less than of the Indians themselves.[4]

A sample data compiled from the Mauritius Archives showed that Indian immigrants purchased 432 pieces of land between 1850 and 1884. The rate of purchase was small up to the 1870s, but increased steadily from one decade to another. The size of land purchased increased from less than 1 arpent (a unit of land measurement where 1 arpent equals 1.043 acres) during the period 1860s and the early 1880s as illustrated in Table 4.1.

Although the data relates to Indians in general, if these facts are mapped on the district of origin of the emigrants who purchased land (Table 4.2), one can find some clarity on emigration through the Calcutta Port. The emigrants who purchased land came from districts such as Arrah, Azamgarh, Gazipur, Benares, etc., for whom Calcutta Port was the only departure point, as in the table.

In Table 4.2, Richard Blair Allen[5] further shows that Indian immigrants who purchased plots in two estates of Mauritius—Terrain Currie and Belle Mare—were neighbours from the same districts in India. The main intention of this purchase was to live with the people who shared the same

TABLE 4.1: Size of Plots Purchased by Indian Immigrants,
1850 –9 to 1880–4

Arpents* (per cent)

Period	Less than 1 Arpent	1–1.9	2–2.9	3–3.9	4–4.9	5–5.9	6–9.9	10 +	Not stated
1850–9	55.6	22.2	8.9	6.7	4.4	2.2	–	–	–
1860–9	70.0	15.7	8.6	2.9	–	1.4	1.4	–	–
1870–9	44.2	28.4	11.6	1.1	3.2	2.1	1.1	4.2	4.2
1880–4	20.3	48.2	16.7	9.9	1.8	1.4	0.5	1.4	–
Average, 1850–84	37.3	35.9	13.4	6.5	2.1	1.6	0.7	1.6	0.9

Source: Blair (1983), 216.

*Arpent: An archaic unit of land measurement composed of 100 perches. Equal to 1.043 acres.

culture, language, and common social organization and social beliefs. In the early years of emigration, labourers arriving in the three West Indian colonies had no intention of staying. Later, once their period of indenture was over, many moved off the estates and tried to establish themselves as independent agriculturists. Rom Ramdin is of the view that 'The gradual

TABLE 4.2: Home Districts of Indian Immigrants Purchasing
Portion of 'Belle Mare' Estate and the Terrain Currie,
1879–84

District	Terrain Currie	'Belle Mare' Estate
Arrah	30 (42.3%)	17 (24.3%)
Azimghur (Azamgarh)	–	2 (2.9%)
Behar (Bihar)	–	1 (1.4%)
Benares	1 (1.4%)	3 (4.3%)
Bhaugulpur (Bhagalpur)	–	1 (1.4%)
Burdwan	3 (4.2%)	–
Chuprah (Chapra)	6 (8.5%)	1 (1.4%)
Gazeepore (Ghazipur)	6 (8.5%)	10 (14.3%)
Guya (Gaya)	5 (7.0%)	8 (11.4%)
Hazareebagh (Hazaribagh)	2 (2.8%)	2 (2.9%)
Midnapore	–	1 (1.4%)
Moonghyr (Monghyr)	1 (1.4%)	1 (1.4%)
Mozufferpore (Muzaffarpur)	1 (1.4%)	–
Patna	1 (1.4%)	5 (7.1%)
Puroolea (Purulia)	5 (7.0%)	1 (1.4%)
Raunchee (Ranchi)	–	3 (4.3%)
Other districts	10 (15.5%)	14 (20.1%)
TOTAL	71	70

Source: Blair (1983), 248.

establishment of an Indian peasantry came about primarily through the land commutation system and through the purchase of Crown lands'. About Trinidad, he proclaimed: 'In 1880, more than ten years after the land commutation scheme was introduced, 2,643 Indian men and their families had been settled on 19,055 acres.'[6]

The proportion of land and landowners increased significantly during the later decades. In an enquiry at Trinidad, James McNeill reported that 'The area of crown land granted to Indians from 1869 to 1876 and from 1885 to 1912 is 89,222 acres. The figures from 1877 to 1884 are not available. . . .'[7] By 1900, in British Guiana, most of the Indians, those eager to settle there, gradually devoted themselves to independent rice cultivation rather than remain attached to sugar estates.[8]

In this context, the Sanderson Commission suggested:

We do not recommend indentured emigration to any colony or Protectorate where there is no agricultural land available for new settlers, or in which it is a condition of the indenture that the labourer should be compelled to return to India on the termination of his contract. The only exception to this rule would be when labourers are engaged in India by the Government of a colony to carry out a special work, such as a railway or canal. Such labourers are, throughout their indenture, practically servants of the State and under the constant care of officers of the Government, and being engaged for a special work may, without objection, be required to return to India on the completion of their engagement.[9]

The effect of indentured Indian immigrant labourers on the sugar colonies was enormous. The skill and techniques used by the labourers introduced improved methods to the cultivation process of those colonies. On the other hand, a large proportion of Indians settled in those colonies, particularly the second and third generations, after meeting their terms indentureship, and established themselves as a resourceful race. The Sanderson Committee Report strengthened this view by adding:

There can be no doubt that in this manner Indian indentured immigration has rendered invaluable service to those of our Colonies in which, on the emancipation of the Negro slaves, the sugar industry was threatened with ruin, or in which a supply of steady labour has been required for the development of the Colony by methods of work to which the native population is averse. The Indian immigration has had a two-fold effect. It has admittedly supplied labour, which could not be obtained in sufficient quantities from other sources. But we were also told by some competent witnesses that according to their observation, in British Guiana and the West Indies at all events, the thrifty and persevering habits of the Indian immigrant have had an educative effect perceptible though gradual, on those among whom he has come to live, and that his example and his competition have introduced new habits of industry and improved methods of agriculture.

It is, moreover, generally admitted that the majority of the Indians who remain in the colony after the expiration of their indentures, either as small proprietors or as free labourers, prove a valuable addition to the population, and that in the second and third generations many inhabitants of Indian extraction become men of considerable property and attainments.[10]

This sequence of events was noticed by George R. Dick, Census Commissioner Mauritius; who in dealing with the results of the Census of 1981 wrote,

One of the noticeable results of the Census which does not appear from the figures and facts borne on the Schedules but was obtained by the observation of the persons engaged in the work, is the existence and development of a peasant proprietary of Indian race or origin; these persons are found to be independent in their manner and conscious of their prosperity and rights.[11]

A considerable proportion of the Indian population in Mauritius not only saved but also learnt to invest their savings in government banks. The annual reports of the Government Savings Banks of Mauritius provided corroborative evidence of the better financial position of Indians in comparison with the Mauritians (or Creoles). In 1851, the average deposit of a Creole agricultural labourer was only £3–6–8 while that of an Indian agricultural labourer was £17–14–4. The aggregate amount deposited by both of these classes during 1851 and 1855 has been recorded in the annual report of the Savings Bank of Mauritius (Table 4.3).

In 1892, the sum of the credit of Indians in the Government Savings Banks of Mauritius was Rs1,526,428.73. This savings amount was possessed by 10,002 persons, which included 235 new immigrants; 6,055

TABLE 4.3: Annual Savings of Mauritian and Indian Agricultural
Class in the Government Savings Banks of Mauritius,
1851, 1855

(Amount in pound)

Year	Class of depositors	
	Mauritian Agricultural	Indian Agricultural
1851	240–2–0	7,919–15–54
1855	190–19–10	13,394–19–2

Source: Blair (1983), 231.

old immigrants; 1,063 passengers* and 2,619 Indo-Mauritians.[12] As the largest portion of the savings belonged to the old immigrants, passengers and the Indo-Mauritians, one can easily conclude that the savings were possible only after the emigrants became free of contract. A reading of the table on savings (Appendix VI) gives an idea of the considerable amount of money that the Indian emigrants brought with them who returned to India from the Four Sugar Colonies. The immigrants from the West Indian colonies like Demerara and Trinidad brought a larger sum of money, signifying that these colonies offered more favourable opportunities.

Noting the return of immigrants coming with considerable capital, Sir Arthur Hobhouse in the Council of the Governor-General, in 1873 said,

[T]hat a very considerable number of them returned to India, bringing with them substantial sums of money; and that of these some—not a very few—were so satisfied with their foreign life that they returned to the colony where they had made their money . . . seem very conclusive proofs that the direct effect of emigration was to improve the welfare of the emigrants. . . .[13]

The emigrant, while staying in the colony, experienced a place free from cholera and famine and found a soil capable of yielding good crops. So he naturally applied to it all his skill and labour and tried to acquire a good fortune. As Grierson pointed out,

[H]e [emigrant] rightly concludes that he has found a place free from cholera and famine, of a warm equable climate, where his natural industry, if rightly applied, makes its possessor in a few years the owner of a large fortune. As there is no competition in this, he is naturally anxious that his friends and relations should share his success. He returns home to his people, and goes back to the colony with several of them, intending this time to settle there for good.[14]

The enhanced state of immigrants and their treatment in the sugar colonies can also be known from the number of re-emigrated Indian labourers (Appendices VII-B and VII-C). These statistical records once again support evidence of the better condition of emigrants in Trinidad and British Guiana (Demerara). In support of this view, Nevil Lubbock quoted testimonies of various authorities who had experienced the system of indentureship in British Guiana and Trinidad. One such evidence is an

---

*Certain persons who proceed to the colonies or other foreign countries without coming under the operation of the Emigration Act, . . . the numbers who leave India as passengers under the Native Passenger Ships Act, or of persons who leave India on pilgrimage to the holy places . . . . (Ferenzi, 1929, pp. 900–1).

extract from the report of Sir James Longden, Governor of British Guiana in 1877, who in his farewell address to British Guiana said, 'The indenture, with the advantages it secures to the Indian coolies, is as necessary for their own protection as it is to guard the interests of the employers'.[15] Lubbock also adds that 'the mortality on the estates is low; a large number of strong and healthy children are growing up, in praise of whose condition the Guiana Commissioner of 1870, spoke strongly. The immigrants are not unfairly worked, and in British Guiana, the average is about four full days in the week'.[16] While narrating the condition of Trinidad, Lubbock forwarded an extract made by the Revd John Morton, a missionary from the Presbyterian Church of Nova Scotia, who said,

A young man who attends one of our schools goes out at 6 o'clock in the morning with his young wife and very frequently walks into schools at 10 o'clock, he and his wife having finished their tasks and earned between them half-crown. Some days they do three tasks between them, earning 3s.6d. and finish by 11 o'clock. After school they cultivate their garden, and nine barrels of rice in husks and six of corn show that their labour is rewarded. . . .[17]

This extract is an observation of the organized life of Indian emigrants in Trinidad.

On 9 July 1914, McNeill and Chimmanlal submitted their report on the condition of Indian immigrants to the secretary to the Government of India, Commerce and Industry department. The report was based on interviews arranged with the heads of the immigration department and other government officers as well as with representatives of the employers of Indian labour and with the Indian associations or individuals of Indian birth or extraction within the colonies and colonial estates. Based on statistical as well as other documentary information, they concluded that after their indentured tenure was over, the Indian emigrants were at par with the rest of the population on the choice of occupation in all the West Indian countries. Compared to Jamaica, the Indian population was large in Trinidad or British Guiana. In British Guiana, about half the total number stayed on estates cultivating plots of land and working on wages. About Trinidad, the report states:

After his five years [in] industrial service an Indian has many choices of occupation. The majority subsist by farming or agricultural labour. All large estates have regular gangs of free Indians who continue to do the same work as that performed during their industrial service. They are housed and given free medical treatment. They are usually under separate headmen and Indian headmen are recruited from their ranks. Some of them are given plots of land on which they grow cane, which is sold to the employer either at a fixed rate or a rate which rises or falls with the market price of sugar. There were over 6,000 Indian cane farmers in 1912.[18]

Immigrants had different avenues of occupation there. Some worked for private employers as gardeners, grooms, porters, watchmen, etc. A fair proportion of them were prosperous traders and a large proportion also owned land.

The Royal Commission's report of 1872 is another crucial source of information on the social and economic history of the Indian immigrant population in Mauritius during the mid-nineteenth century.[19] The main purpose of the Commission was to investigate the charges of ill-treatment and injustice against the Indians and came out with four recommendations:

1. Compulsory work on Sunday should be abolished except attending to animals.
2. Introducing more women from India should alter sex composition of immigrants.
3. Medical treatment for the immigrants should be borne by government.
4. Contract between a new immigrant and his first employer should be reviewed every year and that the governor should have the power to remove immigrants from estate whoever found to be neglecting the law.

The recommendations of the Commission brought about tremendous improvement to the life and condition of the Indian immigrants in Mauritius after 1872 and the progress and development of the immigrants followed a continuous path since then.

Finally, from the percentage of emigrants who never returned, it would be true to say that Trinidad and Demerara were admirably managed and probably the reason why a high percentage settled in those colonies. Grierson, in support, stated that 'between those emigrants who have left India and those who have not returned may hence be taken as representing roughly the popularity of that colony in Hindustan'.[20] Table 4.4 underlines this view: it shows the number of emigrants who went and those who returned from the sugar colonies in each decade. In each decade, more Indian labourers returned from Mauritius as compared to other colonies. The percentage of returned migrants was greater in the last two decades from all the colonies.

TABLE 4.4: Statement Showing the Number of Emigrants through
Calcutta Port who Proceeded to and Returned from Four Sugar Colonies
for the Decades, 1842–70, 1870–80, 1881–90, 1891–1900

Year	Mauritius		Trinidad		Demerara		Jamaica	
	Emigrated to	Returned from	Emigrated to	Retuned from	Emigrated to	Retuned from	Emigrated to	Retuned from
1842–70	351,401*	97,418*	37,527	3,478	68,302	4,048	15,169*	1,818*
1870–80	23,059	9,569	20,813	1,339	45,671	5,326	6,867	1,209
1881–90	7,779	10,845	23,992	4,357	32,659	14,796	1,512	2,875
1891–1900	2,741	2,548	13,440	4,547	20,982	9,701	1,667	721
TOTAL 1870–1900	33,579	22,962	58,245	10,243	99,312	29,823	10,046	4,805

Source: Computed from Geoghagan (1874), General Department Emigration Branch 1871 and from Tables—Appendix I and Appendix IV.

Note: *Data relates to all the three British ports of India. Geoghagan Branch (1874) reports, 'for Mauritius and Jamaica there are no records of Calcutta return migrants'.

Cost of Emigration

India as an emigrant country maintained different policies to prevent the abuses or exploitation of its citizens abroad and provided assistance in case of illness, accident, death, legal trouble or other emergencies. Also, the colonies adopted several measures and services to protect emigrants and effectively utilize these human resources. However, there were some demerits with respect to both the emigrating country and the immigrant colonies:

1. The planters of the sugar colonies desired to retain only the industrious and frugal immigrants. But the actual picture is that the idle vagrant class that earned nothing, or recklessly spent what it earned, was forced to remain in the colony. In order to have an idea of this vagrancy among Indians in those colonies, the figures for the non-productive class are of importance, which are not available. A committee appointed as early as 1880 related to the harbouring of vagrants reported as follows:

Though the committee is of opinion that the population is not in excess of the wants and resources of the colony, it is unfortunately true that there exists in the island [Mauritius] a considerable number of Indians, deserters and others, and of Creoles and Chinese, whose means of existence are uncertain; they constitute a mass of idlers and vagabonds who live almost entirely on the produce of thefts and robberies. Such a class here as elsewhere must be a source of serious evils and anxiety to the community and the government. Here, however, it is beyond doubt that it is the preference for a lazy life, and not the want of opportunities of remunerated work, which drives them into this bad course of life.[21]

The emigration agent for Trinidad (1877) placed instances of corruption and organized crime among Indian immigrants. His report was as follows: 'On the other hand, among the great mass of the coolies there is said to be much drunkenness and want of cleanliness, with a tendency to imitate the lazy habits of the Creole or Negro labourers.' He also forwarded an extract from a report by a Moravian missionary, which stated, 'The most unsatisfactory features are in the coolies' own domestic life and habits, the wife beating, the drunkenness, the apparently almost total absence of religion, and the excessive sharpness of his frugality. . . .'[22]

For Jamaica, a less satisfactory account had been observed:

With a population of half a million, the sugar cultivation remains extremely small. The labour of the island [Jamaica] is either directed to other objects than sugar, or is not productive at all. Vagrancy and squatting increase, and it is sad to see from the statistics of 1876 that there was an increase of crime. The large withdrawals from the savings banks are not to be overlooked. The idle and lawless rob the provision—grounds of the industrious, a practice calculated to take the edge off industry and prevent extension of the class of settlers on whom so much of the future welfare of the island depends.[23]

2. The education of the children of Indian immigrants was a very desirable object, but it was beset by difficulties, especially the difficulty of procuring teachers acquainted with the language of the children. 'While the educational system prevailing in Mauritius provides on the whole well for the Creole population, comparatively little is done as yet for the Indian.'[23]

3. The colonial requirement to have permanent and settled labourers for the estates by enacting a rule on increasing proportion to not less than 40 women to every 100 men for each shipment (General Department, Emigration Branch, June 1877 and November 1881, Resolution) was not as fully complied, as shown in Appendices III-A and III-B.

The statutory proportion of women to men is hardly ever made up without enlisting large numbers of prostitutes, of women of the lowest classes in whom 'habits of honesty and decency' are non-existent.[25]

4. Emigrants were mostly young adults of the age group 20–30 (Table 3.6). Thus, there was a loss of the most energetic human

resources from India, from which the immigration colonies reaped the benefit.

5. Sometimes, recruiters used several tricks to recruit the poor. Helpless and ignorant emigrants in this situation were compelled to follow the recruiters without knowing the terms and conditions, or even their destination. There are several instances of malpractices by the recruiters. The following are some of the evidences:

(a) Proceedings, General Department, June 1871   [No. 7]

    From   C.A. Elliot, Esq., Officiating Secretary to the Government of the NWP

    To   The Secretary to the Government of Bengal, Judicial Department

    (No: 459A, dated Allahabad, the 24th March 1871)

I am directed to forward, for the information of His Honor the Lieutenant-Governor; a copy of the documents . . . quoted, having reference to an attempt made by a recruiter named Buldeo to compel the emigration of some coolies at Allahabad.

I am to inquire whether lists of recruiters are furnished to the Government of Bengal, and what steps are taken to see that proper persons only are employed; and I am at the same time to request that the protector may be called upon the state what connection Bird and Company of Allahabad have with the prisoner Buldeo, and generally as to the principles upon which licenses to recruit are granted in the NWPs.

(b) Proceedings, General Department, September 1871
Ungnoo Versus Seetul, John Manasseh and Luchmun, Sections 416, 343 and 109, Indian Penal Code.

On the 15th a petition was presented in this court by Ungnoo, to the effect that his sister-in-law was detained against her will at the emigration depot in Moteegunge. . . .

I consider this a most serious case; there is no doubt that in many instances women are inveigled on false pretences to the emigration agent's houses, where they are virtually kept prisoners; when they are brought before the Magistrate they are threatened with suits for expenses incurred in feeding them. . . .

The 18th July 1871   J.C. Rovertson
                                          Officiating Magistrate

6. It is clear that India's motive to send people abroad was to ease population pressure and help those who emigrated to seek a decent

livelihood in the immigrant colonies. But the death rate among emigrants during their detention in depots or in sea voyage is a shame to the country.

The mortality rate was high for the emigrants to sugar colonies, especially to the West Indian colonies through Calcutta Port, particularly up to the first half of the decade 1860–70. In total, 4,094 people embarked for the West Indies through Calcutta Port in 1856–7, of which the number of deaths on voyage were 707—indicating a 17.27 per cent mortality rate that year. In a despatch of 22 July 1857, the court of directors drew the attention of the Government of India to the terrible mortality that had attended emigration from Calcutta to the West Indies during the season. For an investigation into its causes, an enquiry 'was ordered to be made, and the Government of Bengal appointed Dr. Mouat to make it'.[26]

Table 4.5 shows the mortality rate on the voyage from Calcutta to the Mauritian and West Indian colonies during 1859–70. The mortality rate is highest among the emigrants to British Guiana as compared to other colonies, as the colony's depot was located on the banks of the polluted Hooghly, due to which many diseases killed emigrants. On the issue, Geogeghan in his report commented:

We have already seen the terrible mortality of the year 1856, when 17.27 percent of the emigrants sailing for the West Indies from Calcutta perished on the voyage. In 1857, the mortality still stood at the high figure of 13.22 percent; in 1858, it was reduced to 10.43 percent, and in the following year rose again to 12.6. It then was considerably reduced till the fatal year 1864, when one-fourth of the emigrants from Calcutta to British Guiana died on the Voyage.

It was suggested in 1858 that perhaps the large number of 'hill coolies' shipped from Calcutta was one of the main causes of the heavy mortality of the Bengal emigration to the West Indies of the years 1856 to 1858, and it is an undoubted fact that this class does suffer greatly even on board river steamers. But this would not explain the great sickness of 1864, for, owing to the competition of the tea districts, the number of Dhangars, Kols and their congeners, sailing to the West Indies, had greatly diminished. Altogether the question is distressingly obscure.[27]

With the introduction of steamships, the duration of the sea journey reduced to almost half, which may be the primary cause for reduction in the mortality rate (particularly to Demerara during the 1880s (Table 4.6) as compared to 1860s, as shown in Table 4.5. On the other hand, mortality at the depot decreased due to reduction in various diseases since 1877–8 (see Appendix VIII).

TABLE 4.5: Percentage of Mortality on the Voyage from Calcutta to Mauritius, Demerara, Trinidad and Jamaica during 1859–1870

Year	Voyage from Calcutta to			
	Mauritius	Demerara	Trinidad	Jamaica
1859	–	13.4	9.4	19.9
1860	3.3	3.7	6.9	11.8
1861	1.9	4.6	3.5	8.8
1862	1.8	3.0	2.8	–
1863	1.7	3.3	3.2	–
1864	1.6	25.1	3.0	–
1865	3.2	6.6	10.8	–
1866	0.6	3.8	4.1	4.9
1867	1.0	3.3	2.6	–
1868	1.5	3.3	2.6	–
1869	0.2	4.6	1.7	2.6
1870	1.0	1.2	2.1	1.6

Source: Computed from the Report of Geogeghan, 1874, pp. 73, 75.

Apart from sea voyage, in the early forties, a heavy workload, unaccustomed with the new land and harsh treatment from the employers was also responsible for the high mortality among the Indian workers. This can be confirmed from the following paragraphs:

During the early years of emigration, the mortality among the immigrants was due to the lack of realization among them about the condition of their new life. The report of the Commissioners of Enquiry into the condition and treatment of Immigrants in British Guiana discloses that 'As yet inexperienced in the country, unbroken to the labour, and

TABLE 4.6: Percentage of Mortality in the Vessel among the Emigrants Carried to the Sugar Colonies from 1883–4 to 1889–90

Year	Colonies to which Vessels were Bound			
	Mauritius	Demerara	Trinidad	Jamaica
1883–4	1.32	1.01	–	1.30
1884–5	2.97	2.51	4.67	0.29
1885–6	2.11	0.78	–	–
1886–7	1.08	0.95	–	–
1887–8	1.38	1.27	–	–
1888–9	1.68	0.97	–	–
1889–1990	1.43	2.69	–	0.40

Source: Computed from Proceedings, General Department. Annual Report, 1883–4 to 1889–90.

unacclimatized, they took helplessly to a wondering life, and succumbed to the hardships of it without care and without pity'. About the condition of Trinidad which was more worse, the report added an extract from Lord Harris, the Governor of Trinidad, who wrote in 1848 that 'scarcely a week passes, but reports are sent in from different parts of the colony of the skeletons of coolies being found in the woods and cane pieces'.[28]

The Truth and Justice Commission was established in Mauritius in 2009 to investigate the history and consequences of slavery and indenture during the colonial period. While inquiring the reality of the treatment against the indentured Indians after the resumption of Immigration to the island in the early forties, the report says, '. . . there was still much room for abuse: wages were on the low side, housing conditions were poor and hours of work unregulated. Indian immigrant who refused to renew their employment contract with the same employers were arrested under vagrancy laws, imprisoned and inflicted corporal punishment'.[29]

However, this cost–benefit analysis of emigration and the key question related to outweighing them remains a matter of debate and will be concluded in the last chapter.

Notes

1. Moses D.E. Nwulia, *The History of Slavery in Mauritius and the Seychelles, 1810–1875*, London: Associated University Press, 1981, p. 189.
2. J.W.P. Muir-Mackenzie, 'Report on the Condition of Indian Immigrants in Mauritius', General Department, Emigration Branch, Government of Bengal, Calcutta: WBSA, July 1895, p. 18.
3. Nevil Lubbock, 'Present Position of the West Indian Colonies', Read at a meeting of the Royal Colonial Institute, London, General Department, Emigration Branch, Government of Bengal, Calcutta: WBSA, July 1877, p. 5.
4. Sanderson Commission, 'Report of the Committee on Emigration from India to the Crown Colonies and Protectorates, PP, Great Britain, vol. XXVII, 1910.
5. Richard Blair Allen, 'Creoles, Indian Immigrants and the Restructuring of Society and Economy in Mauritius, 1767–1885', unpublished Ph.D. dissertation, Michigan: University of Illinois, 1983, p. 248.
6. Rom Ramdin, *Arising from Bondage: A History of the Indo-Caribbean People*, London: I.B.Tauris Publishers, 2000, p. 86.
7. James McNeill and Chimmanlal, *Report on the Condition of Indian Immigrants in the Four British Colonies: Trinidad, British Guiana or Demerara, Jamaica and Fiji and in the Dutch Colony of Surinam or Dutch Guiana*, Simla: Government Central Press (Government of India), 1914, p. 40.
8. Ramdin, *Arising from Bondage*, p. 68.
9. Sanderson Commission, 'Report of the Committee on Emigration from India to the Crown Colonies and Protectorates'.

10. Ibid.
11. Census of Mauritius and its dependencies taken on 6 April 1891, Mauritius. The Central Punting Establishment, 1892.
12. Muir-Mackenzie, 'Condition of Indian Immigrants in Mauritius', p. 52.
13. Lubbock, 'Present Position of the West Indian Colonies', p. 5.
14. George A. Grierson, 'Report on Colonial Emigration from the Bengal Presidency', General Department, Emigration Branch, Appendix A, File 15–20/21, Government of Bengal, Calcutta: WBSA, June 1883, p. 35.
15. Lubbock, 'Present Position of the West Indian Colonies', p. 6.
16. Ibid.
17. Ibid., p. 42.
18. McNeill and Chimmanlal, *The Condition of Indian Immigrants in the Four British Colonies*, p. 40.
19. K. Hazareesingh, *History of Indians in Mauritius*, London: Macmillan Education, 1975, p. 52.
20. Grierson, 'Report on Colonial Emigration from the Bengal Presidency', p. 40.
21. Muir-Mackenzie, 'Condition of Indian Immigrants in Mauritius', p. 43.
22. Govternment of Bengal, 'The Report of the Protector of Emigrants to British and Foreign Colonies during the year ending 31st March 1878', Resolution, General Department, Emigration Branch, Calcutta: WBSA, September 1878, p. 204.
23. Lubbock, 'Present Position of the West Indian Colonies', p. 43.
24. Muir-Mackenzie, 'Condition of Indian Immigrants in Mauritius', p. 49.
25. Government of Bengal, 'On the subject of the revision of the system of emigration from India to British and Foreign Colonies', General Department, Emigration Branch, Proceeding, Calcutta: WBSA, September 1879, p. 7.
26. Great Britain, J. Geoghegan, (Esq., Under Secretary to the Government of India, Department of Agriculture, Revenue and Commerce), 'Note on Coolie Emigration from India', PP, vol. XLVII, 1874, p. 26.
27. Ibid., p. 76.
28. 'The Report of the Commissioners of Enquiry into the Condition and Treatment of Immigrants in British 'Guiana', PP, vol. XX, 1871, p. 40.
29. Report of the Truth and Justice Commission, Mauritius, vol. I, 2011, printed by Government Punting (www.usip.org/sites/default/files/ROL/TSC vol. I.pdf).

SUPPORTING DOCUMENTS

Proceedings, General Department, 23rd June 1859

[No. 24] From Captain John G. Reddie, Protector of Emigrants at Calcutta
        To   A.R. Young, Esq., Secretary to the Government of Bengal
           (No. 14, dated the 16th June 1859)

. . . I am of opinion that Emigration to Mauritius and West Indies is most popular and that coolies have returned after a few years with large sum of money in their possession and very few without any means. Coolies are in the habit of coming back to India and after a sojourn of a few months amongst their families and friends, again emigrate accompanied by a number of their village people; their general appearance is robust and healthy and they seem to have greatly improved by their intercourse in the colonies; they also appear to have acquired independent ideas and European habits, which they endeavour to instill into their Country people. . . .

The demand for Coolies both from West Indies and Mauritius are very much on the increase.

Proceedings, General Department, Emigration Branch, March 1862, Page 25

[No. 24]   From   Captain C. Eales, Protector of Emigrants at the Port of Calcutta.

          To   H. Bell, Esq., Officiating Junior Secretary to the Government of Bengal (No. 69, dated the 1st March 1862)

I have the honour to report the arrival at Calcutta, on the 21st ultimo, of the ship Brechin Castle, T. Watterston, Master, 537 tons, from the Island of Trinidad on the 24th October, and the Cape of Good Hope on the 28th December last, with the under mentioned number of returned emigrants and Topazes:

Return Emigrants, etc.	Numerical list					
	Men	Women	Boys	Girls	Infants	Total
Embarked on the 23rd October 1861	240	34	10	17	6	307 souls
Born during the voyage	–	–	–	–	1	
Died during the voyage	17	2	–	–	–	
Arrival in Port	223	32	10	17	7	289 souls including eleven topazes

The Money Savings amassed by these Coolies amount in the aggregate to £4,186–0–11, of which £2,692–1–9 was remitted overland to the Emigration Agent by Bills and 6,499 Dollars, and loose cash equivalent to £1,493–19–2, were brought in the ship under the charge of the Surgeon.

The people were questioned as to the sufficiency of food and water issued to them, and the treatment experienced on board, and expressed themselves perfectly

Return Emigrants, etc.	Numerical list					
	Men	Women	Boys	Girls	Infants	Total
Embarked on the 23rd October 1861	240	34	10	17	6	307 souls
Born during the voyage	–	–	–	–	1	
Died during the voyage	17	2	–	–	–	
Arrival in Port	223	32	10	17	7	289 souls including eleven topazes

satisfied. The provisions of the Charter Party have been fully and fairly complied with. They were particularly cautioned against the danger of travelling with loose cash upon their persons.

Proceedings, General Department, Emigration Branch, March 1862, Page 25

[No. 24]   From   Captain C. Eales, Protector of Emigrants at the Port of Calcutta
            To   H. Bell, Esq., Officiating Junior Secretary to the Government of Bengal (No. 90, dated the 11th March 1862)

I have the honour to report the arrival, at Calcutta on the 7th instant, of the ship Shah Alum, Tullock, Master, 579 Tons, from the Island of Mauritius, on the 17th January last, with the under mentioned number of returned Emigrants, Invalids, Topazes, and Cooks.

The people were mustered on arrival, and their names and numbers corresponded with a duplicate Nominal Roll in the possession of the Commandar. They were questioned as to the sufficiency of food and water issued to them, and the treatment experienced on board, and expressed themselves perfectly satisfied. They were likewise cautioned against the danger of travelling with loose cash upon their persons.

Proceedings, General Department, Emigration Branch, June 1871

[No. 8]   From   The Revd Thomas Evans, Missionary
           To   The Hon'ble Sir William Muir, K.C.S.I., Lieutenant Governor, NWPs (dated Allahabad, the 18th February 1871)

A painful revelation was made to me here yesterday, which I deem of sufficient importance to communicate for your information.

About 9 o'clock yesterday morning, a man by name Ganga, who has worked for me as mochi off and on for the last three years, came here in great distress, and gave me the following story:-

He said that his chichi (aunt) went on Tuesday last in search of work, when she met a chupprassee, who asked her if she would grind some corn, and be paid for it. She said she would, and followed the man. He took her to a place in Khoordabad (near Khoosroo Bagh) and put her to sit down with some women, saying they would get work in a little while. Latter in the day she with others get some food to eat, and having eaten, were told that now their names would be written 'by the orders of the Sirkar' to go to 'Miritch desh' (Mauritius) as coolies, where they would get plenty of good food and nice cloths, etc.

They all protested and begged hard to be let go, but to no purpose. . . . Ganga mochi came to me, as I said, and begged of me with tears to try and get the women his liberty. Having examined him well, I told him to meet me at Khoordabad by 12 noon, . . .

I saw in all about ten or eleven women there, and asked who had charge of them. A peon present said he had, but that the head man was Buldeo Jamadar, who had gone out, . . . I now asked each one of them how they came there, and they had all but one tale to tell, which quite corresponded with what the mochi had told me about his aunt . . . In about half an hour Buldeo came, . . . I again said, 'How came they here and are they kept here against their will?' He said, 'Oh no'. 'Well', said I, 'may they go away if they wish?' 'Yes' said he, 'they may'. I then called two men to witness this (i.e. Ganga Sing Jamadar and Bukhtawar Khan, who said he was servent to Mr. Webb), and I said, 'Will you two witness to what this man says, and to what I will ask these women, and to what they will answer?' I then asked each woman before all 'Are you or are you not, willing to stay here?' They all said, 'No sahib, we are not; we are kept here by force against our will, and we beg of you in the name of God to let us go.' 'Well', said I, 'this man says you may go if you wish; so go.'

When Buldeo saw they were gone, he got into a great rage, and said he would go and report to the 'burra Sahib'. I asked him who is 'burra Sahib' was, when he said 'Bird Company.'. . . They [Bird Company] expressed their sorrow for the way in which Buldeo decoyed the women. . . . My first impulse was to go direct to the magistrate and inform him. I then thought the Pioneer, but on further reflection I thought it would be best of all to write and inform you, as that may prove the most effectual method of putting down such cruelty.

Proceedings, General Department, Emigration Branch, April 1872

Suicide among Indian Labourers in the Mauritius

[4] No. 102, dated Downing Street, the 9th June 1871
   From The Right Hon'ble the Earl of Kinberley
   To Sir A. Gordon, K.C.M.G., Governor of Mauritius

With reference to my dispatch No. 84 dated the 19th November last, I transit to you, for your consideration, the copy of a letter, with its enclosures, from the India Office, respecting the frequency of the Crime of Suicide among the Indian immigrants in Mauritius.

I request you to make some further investigation into this matter as soon as the necessary data are procured.

I would call your attention to the statement contained in the extract from the annals of Indian administration in the year 1866–67, supplied by the Government of Bengal, to the effect that 'the most common causes of suicide in India are jealousy, family discord, destitution, and physical suffering'; and I have to request you to cause the records of corner's inquests on suicides for the last five years to be examined, in order to ascertain what proportion of them may be attributable to jealousy or family discord.

Proceedings, General Department,
Emigration Branch, April 1872

Suicide among Indian Labourers in the Mauritius

[5] No. 118, dated Mauritius, the 28th July 1871
    From   Sir A. Gordon, K.C.M.G., Governor of Mauritius
    To   The Right Hon'ble the Earl of Kimberley

I shall of course inquire much more closely into these curious discrepancies which, whatever their cause, deprive both returns of much of their value.

Whichever set however we regard as the most trustworthy, the number of suicides is very large indeed, and I fear we must consider the heavier return to be the truer one; for whilst many suicides may well escape the notice of the police, or not to be reported to the Civil Status, it is almost impossible that deaths should be registered as suicides if not really due to that cause.

Out of the 642 suicides reported to the police in the ten years ending 31st December, 1870, only 83 are attributed to jealousy, 26 to revenges, 28 to poverty, 189 to sickness, 82 to temporary insanity, 17 to ill treatment, and 217 to unknown causes.

Here, suicides are almost all those of males, only 17 suicides of women having occurred out of a total of 642, according to the police, or 29 out of a total of 577, according to the Civil Status.

I myself believe that a very large portion of these suicides are due to nostalgia or an intense desire to return to India, which they have no means of gratifying.

The whole subject, however, is one which calls for further inquiry, and will not be neglected by me.

Proceedings, General Department,
Emigration Branch, February 1876

Annual Report on Emigration to British and Foreign Colonies
for the year ending 31st March 1875, Page 55

No. 1391C, dated Calcutta, the 15th November 1875, File 25–13/14
    From   J.G. Grant, Esq., M.D., Protector of Emigrants, Calcutta
    To   The Officiating Under Secretary to the Government of Bengal

I have the honour to submit, for the information of Government, my annual report on emigration to British and foreign Colonies for the year ending March 1875.

Return Emigration (Page 63)

The following table gives the number of emigrants who returned from the several colonies noted below, and some particulars as to the amount of their savings and death rate on the passage:

Colonies	No. of Ships	No. of Souls	Average % of mortaliy	Savings					
				Aggregate amounts Average amounts			Average amounts		
				Rs.	A.	P.	Rs.	A.	P.
Mauritius	6	1,837	0.65	181,206	0	0	98	10	3
Demerara	2	900	3.33	163,291	2	4	181	6	11
Trinidad	1	405	2.41	106,635	14	0	263	4	9

Proceedings, General Department, Emigration Branch, August 1877

Eighteenth Annual Report of the Protector of Emigrants at Mauritius for the year 1876

From   T. Elliott, acting Protector of immigrants
To   The Hon'ble the Acting Colonial Secretary &c &c

Statement of Amounts of money declared by immigrants leaving the colony in 1876

Amount declared (in rupees)			
Men	1,030	Gold	25,711
Women	280	silver	153,904
Children	230	Drafts	49,240
TOTAL			228,855
Number of men who declared nothing			196

Amount of savings declared by coolies who left the colony in 1856 to Calcutta

Under 50 rupees	125
Under 100 rupees	106
Under 150 rupees	132
Under 200 rupees	115
Under 250 rupees	102
Under 300 rupees	68
Under 350 rupees	50
Under 400 rupees	40
Under 500 rupees	49
Under 1,000 rupees	79
Under 2,000 rupees	19
Under 3,200 rupees	2
Under 4,600 rupees	1
TOTAL	888

Total amount of savings declared by coolies who left the colony to

Madras	428
Bombay	163
Other places	7

Total including Calcutta   1,486

Proceeding, General Department, September 1878

App.b File 89—2 RESOLUTION

The Emigration Agent for Trinidad has placed on record some remarkable instances of the success of Indian Immigrants in that colony, and forwards an extract from a report by a Moravian Missionary furnishing satisfactory evidence for the material prosperity of immigrants in Demerara.

The following extract from a report made by the Reverend Henry Mooro a Morevian Missionary, has been sent to me by Mr Firth the Emigration agent for Demerara.

There can be no doubt that the coolies in Demerara are very happy as happy as they care to be happier, certainly, than such as those in their own country could possible be. They are provided with neat and comfortable cottages, they obtain good wages—from 1s. to 4s. Per Diem. They can save money, and they do. They buy cattle. The coolie is presumed to be able to save at the least an average sum of one dollar a week. In six or eight months after his arrival in the colony he purchases his cow, he sells his milk to the estate hospital, or in the town; he rears up calves and other live stock, he prospers, and soon he has an account at the savings bank. He is treated kindly by the estate authorities. He is far from being in serfdom or semi-serfdom. Should be feel aggrieved; there are Government immigration Officials to whom he does not hesitate to apply. He has his schools, his hospital, his doctor, his missionary. Those in England of the anti-slavery party who complain of the bad treatment of the unsatisfactory condition of the coolies, need but to come and live for a few days near any coolie village on either of the plantations, to learn that the condition of the coolie is comfortable, and their treatment by the estate authorities all that could be desired. There is no such thing as planter oppression and injustice towards them. The most unsatisfactory features are in the coolies' own domestic life and habits, the wife beating, the drunkenness, the apparently almost total absence of religion, and the excessive sharpness of his frugality. One would like to see them more cleanly and adopting in their personal appearance a little more extensively the habits and customs of civilized life. They are in many respects an interesting people, and the more closely one comes into contact with them, the more one gets to appreciate them, and to realize the services that they render to the country and the services the country renders them. Many even of the coolies are complained as being lazy, adopting the habit, in that respect, of the natives, from whom it is said the Barbadians contracted it; many of the coolies scarcely even work on Mondays and do very little on Tuesdays.

The above facts appear to be testify not only to the industry and providence of many of the emigrants, but to the favourable nature of the terms under which they emigrate to certain colonies.

Proceedings, General Department, Emigration Branch, March 1882

No. 311, dated Calcutta, the 14th March 1882
      From   J.G.G. Grant, Esq., Protector of Emigrants
      To   The Offg. Under Secretary to the Government of Bengal, General Department

I have the honour to acknowledge . . . calling for a return, for the last three (official) years showing the total sum remitted to India each year by Indian emigrants from each of the several colonies to which emigration is allowed and the number of emigrants making the remittances.

Statement of remittances to India from the Colonies during the years 1878–79 to 1880–1

Proceedings, General Department, Emigration Branch, May 1890

No. 4621, dated Calcutta, the 19th December, 1889
      From   Surgeon Major P.W.D. Comins, M.D., Protector of Emigrants, Calcutta
      To   The Secretary to the Government of Bengal, General Department

. . . Apart from the benefits direct and indirect, derived by India from Colonial Emigration by the relief of overpopulated districts, the provision of profitable labour for an indigent section of the population, and also the return to India of a well-to-do class of labourers with earnings often of large amount of whom they have returned yesterday in the ship Erne emigrants bringing with them earnings to the value of about one and a half lakhs of rupees, all of which will be spent in India, there are two sources of income which, though not so accredited, may fairly be counted as assets of Colonial Emigration. They are the income derived from the sale of stamps for licenses of emigrant vessels, which amounted during the year to Rs.1,071, and that accruing from deceased emigrants' estates, the heirs to which cannot be traced. From this source there was credited last year in the Government accounts Rs.1,707–7–11.

Statement of Remittences to India from the Colonies during the Years 1878–9 to 1880–1

Colonies	1878–9										1979–80										1980–1										Total of the three years									
	No. of remitters	Amount of remittance				Average amount remitted by each emigrant					No. of remitters	Amount of remittance				Average amount remitted by each emigrant					No. of remitters	Amount of remittance				Average amount remitted by each emigrant					No. of remitters	Amount of remittance				Average amount remitted by each emigrant			
		Rs.	A.	P.		Rs.	A.	P.				Rs.	A.	P.		Rs.	A.	P.				Rs.	A.	P.		Rs.	A.	P.				Rs.	A.	P.		Rs.	A.	P.	
Demerara	27	2,273	15	8		84	3	6		82		5,299	2	7		64	9	11		135		5,734	8	7		42	7	7		244		13,307	10	10		54	8	7	
Trinidad	22	2,269	12	8		103	2	9		462		130,013	13	9		281	6	7		448		152,677	7	2		340	12	9		932		284,961	1	7		305	12	0	
Jamaica	223	24,270	2	3		109	11	8		372		48,129	8	0		129	6	1		356		59,085	7	2		165	15	6		951		131,685	1	5		138	7	3	
Mauritius	180	71,931	0	0		399	9	3		204		87,600	0	0		429	6	7		144		57,549	0	0		399	10	4		528		217,080	0	0		411	2	2	

5

Conclusion

LABOUR EMIGRATION IS THE transportation of the most valuable economic resource—human capital—across the seas. The family, local community and the state of origin bear the cost of raising a migrant to young adulthood and the immigration country reaps the benefit of this investment. A thorough scrutiny of various records and data analysis corroborated with the fact that Indian labourers pushed out for emigration to the sugar colonies were mostly from famine-striven, drought and flood-affected areas and were those people who had passed long periods of semi-starvation. The institution of slavery was abolished in the British Empire with the Act of Emancipation of 1834. Succumbing to pressure by the plantation owners worldwide, the British colonial authorities introduced the system of indentured Indian immigration, and it was believed that government controlled recruitment and shipping could be more efficiently supervised by a government agent at Calcutta. Thus, since the mid-nineteenth century, and continuing up to the early twentieth century, there emerged a relationship between the planter and the indentured.

Throughout the nineteenth century, Calcutta Port remained the busiest port in colonial India, providing passage to emigrant labourers from India to the four sugar colonies, viz., Mauritius, British Guiana, Trinidad and Jamaica. The many facets of Calcutta port have been discussed in each chapter and deserve a comment here.

For over 100 years, many people were displaced internally—within the Indian subcontinent—and externally—overseas. As Haraprasad Chattopadhyay observed, 'probably not before the 19th century had so many of our brothers and sisters migrated to distant overseas countries where to begin a new life in quite an unfamiliar environment . . .'.[1] Official records of emigration from Calcutta date back to 1837, but from 1842 onwards—only a few years after the abolition of slavery in British sugar colonies—the records became more regular. To this effect, a committee appointed by the Parliament recommended the emigration.

In connection with the large flow of emigrants during the period 1842–1900, when around 70 per cent of indentured labour migrated through Calcutta port alone, the natural question invariably arose whether those people from the Gangetic plains were normally inclined to such mobility or forced to move.

The economic circumstances of the famine-striven areas overwhelmingly favoured the emigration agents for collecting labour at the cheapest rate from Calcutta Port. Colonial emigration was only one of many vents for unemployed labourers in India. Mr Grierson pointed out that 'the bulk of people registered there (at Alipur, Calcutta) are up-country men who have come down to Calcutta look for work, and have failed to find it.'[2] Those poor villagers were then deceived and registered for indentured labour in colonies. Records show that these emigrants came largely from a few zones or pockets of India: Bihar, Bengal, North-Western Provinces and Oudh, the major emigration centres supplying unskilled labourers to overseas sugar colonies. These were also the common areas of inland migration for factory work around Calcutta and the surrounding industrial districts of Bengal during the years 1891 and 1901 and onwards. The most noticeable feature of emigration to the colonies was the great demand for labour in Mauritius and Demerara (British Guiana) during the whole period, and mostly through the Calcutta port (Appendix I). Another striking aspect is the popularity of Demerara and Trinidad as emigration destinations over the other two colonies.

The socio-economic conditions of the immigrant labourers in those colonies became favourable from the 1870s onwards. This is evident from the growth of the Indian population in the four colonies. Once, the stipulated tenure of labour was over, the immigrant labourer was a free person, worthy of equal rights to select a way of income and hold land. The Indian diaspora soon acquired capital through savings and land.

To encourage emigrants and emigration, Grierson added (a measure to the Emigration Act of 1871) that

surely emigration may also be looked upon as an engine of immense power for good to India. The more safety-valve there are for a pent up population in time of famine, the greater chance there will be of saving life, and if I may venture to offer an opinion on such a point, I maintain strongly that it is Government's imperative duty to actively encourage emigration by every legitimate means in its power, and to let it be known far and wide that the Emigration Department is a Government one.[3]

From the earlier abridgement of major observations and findings and their relationship to the purpose of this research, we make the following conclusions.

From an economic point of view, before 1838, the British West Indies and Mauritius had no link, of trade or otherwise, with India. The factors that linked these sugar colonies to the Indian peninsula were: abolishment of slavery and the near collapse of the agricultural economy in those colonies, and the introduction of the indenture system that worked well with the Indians who were brought into the colonies in greater numbers than from any other countries.

It was not only the colonies that benefited from the cheap immigrant labourers who restored their sugar plantations. For the poor and landless Indian peasants, emigration was a way out of their famine-struck environment. In addition, the freedom to exercise their rights after indenture helped the emigrants become prosperous settlers. However, presence of idlers and vagabonds among the indentured. Indians in the colonies, who live almost entirely on the produce of theft and robberies, became a serious cause of anxiety to the community and the government there. Nonetheless, the greatest loss for India was the loss of the most energetic human resource—young adults in the age group 20–30.

From the standpoint of the Indians, the fundamental cause of emigration to overseas was linked to environmental factors like flood, famine, drought and crop failure, compelling them to leave their homeland for survival and a better life. However, other economic factors like the loss of land rights, poverty, indebtedness and unemployment and social factors like high population density, overcrowding and castism also acted as push factors.

In addition to the challenges that Indian labourers faced at the end of their indentureship—moving from the estates and attempting to establish themselves as independent agriculturists—this development brought them in direct conflict with the planters. In the early days of colonization, the planters had maintained silence on any issue regarding race discrimination due to the need for indentured labour—their only objective was to maintain a supply of continuous cheap labour. The cost of return passage as well as that of replacement hit their interests and they objected to the freedom given to Indians to own savings fearing drainage of wealth from their countries to India. Nonetheless, the negative side of the planters' objectives raised concern among Indian nationalists who led the anti-indentureship campaign and helped put an end to the system.

Thus, one cannot deny the truth that the upsurge of nationalism among the Indians and the emergence of independence was a direct consequence of the long period of misery and suffering of the emigrants under indentureship. Investigations also discloses that in reality among the large number of emigrants who deliberately left their own districts for colonies, during the mutiny years 1857–9, a part of suspected mutineer sepoys were also transported, who in the subsequent years may have raised the feelings of freedom and rights among the indentured Indians settled there.[4] This view has been supported in a study that stated: 'Paradoxically the return of Indians to their own country enriched with their savings, with new skills and experience was one of the contributing factors to Indian restlessness under alien government and to the rapid appearance of nationalism and a growing demand for independence'.[5]

In the final analysis, it can be concluded that the twin issues of cost of emigration and benefit from emigration are interlinked. Under indentureship, the poor but hardworking Indians, whether landless labourers or the sons of poor cultivating landowners, achieved more in the Caribbean than they could have hoped to achieve in their homeland. However, it is also true that experience of the abusive practices and severe treatment by the planters during their indentureship brought long term impact on the Indian society at colonies. Recruitment of efficient emigrants became difficult during the later decades of the nineteenth century in part due to the improvement in communication and also due to the industrial revival in India, which opened up a larger field of earning opportunity within the country, especially in Bengal and its industrial districts. Wage rate in factories and mills around Calcutta was comparatively higher than the agricultural work which attached migrants more to their homeland while in depot. As such, all recruitment agencies that caused controlled emigration began to gradually close up as migrants turned their sights homewards with a dream of a much better, new and free life.

Notes

1. Haraprasad Chattopadhyay, *Internal Migration in India: A Case Study of Bengal* (Covering the period from the second half of the 19th century till the Census year 1931), Calcutta: K.P. Bagchi & Company, 1987, p. 17.
2. George A. Grierson, 'Report on Colonial Emigration from the Bengal Presidency', General Dept., Emigration Branch, Appendix A, File 15–20/21, Govt. of Bengal, Calcutta: WBSA, June 1883, p. 1.
3. Ibid., p. 18.

4. See for a fuller discussion of the role of mutineers on the Indian Emigrants to Mauritius Castes, Marina and Crispin Bates, 'Empire and Locality: A Global Dimension to the 1857 Indian Uprising, *Journal of Colombo History*, vol. 5, 2010, p. 51.

5. I.M. Cumpston, *Indians Overseas in British Territories, 1834–1854*, London: OUP, 1953, p. 179.

Appendices

APPENDIX I

Gross Emigration from British India to Four Sugar Colonies and through Calcutta Port, 1842–1900

Year	Mauritius			Trinidad			Demerara			Jamaica		
	Total Emigration	Through Calcutta Port	Percentage to Total	Total Emigration	Through Calcutta Port	Percentage to Total	Total Emigration	Through Calcutta Port	Percentage to Total	Total Emigration	Through Calcutta Port	Percentage to Total
1842	459	459	100.00	–	–	–	–	–	–	–	–	–
1843	39,755	17,653	44.41	–	–	–	–	–	–	–	–	–
1844	8,242	7,171	87.00	–	–	–	–	–	–	–	–	–
1845	8,541	8,542	100.00	1,332	1,332	100.00	1,591	1,359	85.42	1,047	1,047	100.00
1846	7,180	7,180	100.00	2,264	755	33.35	4,901	1,416	28.89	2,390	780	32.65
1847	5,933	5,813	97.98	1,236	619	50.08	2,372	1,519	64.04	1,178	540	45.84
1848	5,780	5,667	98.05	680	680	100.00	3,211	1,024	31.89	–	–	–
1849	7,670	7,585	98.89	–	–	–	–	–	–	–	–	–
1850	9,800	5,944	60.65	–	–	–	–	–	–	–	–	–
1851	11,245	6,948	61.79	1,094	1,094	100.00	1,927	1,927	100.00	–	–	–
1852	18,594	7,994	43.00	1,729	1,729	100.00	2,351	2,351	100.00	–	–	–
1853	15,631	10,218	65.37	1,497	1,497	100.00	2,653	2,653	100.00	–	–	–
1854	16,712	8,590	51.40	294	294	100.00	2,321	2,321	100.00	–	–	–
1855	15,057	8,229	54.65	623	623	100.00	949	949	100.00	–	–	–
1856	9,751	3,533	36.21	1,561	1,561	100.00	2,879	1,983	68.88	–	–	–

(Contd.)

Appendix I (*contd.*)

Year	Mauritius			Trinidad			Demerara			Jamaica		
	Total Emigration	Through Calcutta Port	Percentage to Total	Total Emigration	Through Calcutta Port	Percentage to Total	Total Emigration	Through Calcutta Port	Percentage to Total	Total Emigration	Through Calcutta Port	Percentage to Total
1857	17,117	11,250	65.72	1,451	1,451	100.00	1,855	1,091	58.81	–	–	–
1858	38,735	22,499	58.08	3,619	2,173	60.04	2,839	2,462	86.72	–	–	–
1859	33,927	17,606	51.89	2,526	1,736	68.73	4,939	4,594	93.01	703	703	100.00
1860	11,603	6,091	52.50	2,710	2,080	76.75	5,229	4,288	82.00	1,709	1,709	100.00
1861	14,182	6,936	48.91	2,030	2,030	100.00	5,386	4,366	81.06	2,161	2,161	100.00
1862	8,322	2,284	27.45	1,389	1,389	100.00	3,326	2,967	89.21	544	N.A.	–
1863	5,548	1,822	32.84	1,433	1,433	100.00	2,643	2,643	100.00	–	–	–
1864	10,607	6,868	64.75	1,450	1,450	100.00	3,139	3,139	100.00	–	–	–
1865	19,493	1,51,157	77.54	1,498	1,498	100.00	2,842	2,842	100.00	–	–	–
1866	3,549	478	13.47	2,993	2,993	100.00	4,509	4,509	100.00	1,705	1,705	100.00
1867	313	313	100.00	1,840	1,840	100.00	3,001	3,001	100.00	–	–	–
1868	1,595	1,237	77.55	2,248	2,248	100.00	4,944	5,014	100.00	1,426	1,426	100.00
1869	2,787	1,499	53.79	2,935	2,935	100.00	6,685	6,685	100.00	924	924	100.00
1870–1	3,273	1,937	59.18	2,087	2,087	100.00	3,199	3,199	100.00	1,382	1,382	100.00
1871–2	4,321	2,990	69.20	N.A.	1,620	–	2,125	2,125	100.00	N.A.	1,426	100.00
1872–3	6,816	5,262	77.20	N.A.	2,850	–	6,087	6,087	100.00	N.A.	1,562	100.00
1873–4	7,725	5,387	69.73	N.A.	2,138	–	8,497	8,497	100.00	N.A.	1,463	100.00
1874–5	6,800	4,914	72.26	N.A.	2,540	–	3,942	3,942	100.00	N.A.	1,258	100.00
1875–6	1,033	739	71.54	N.A.	1,653	–	3,849	3,849	100.00	N.A.	767	100.00
1876–7	1,027	1,027	100.00	N.A.	1,601	–	3,992	3,992	100.00	1,163	N.A.	–
1877–8	3,836	2,034	53.02	N.A.	2,151	–	8,288	8,288	100.00	N.A.	896	–

(*Contd.*)

Appendix I (contd.)

Year	Mauritius			Trinidad			Demerara			Jamaica		
	Total Emigration	Through Calcutta Port	Percentage to Total	Total Emigration	Through Calcutta Port	Percentage to Total	Total Emigration	Through Calcutta Port	Percentage to Total	Total Emigration	Through Calcutta Port	Percentage to Total
1878–9	3,647	1,220	33.45	2,632	2,632	100.00	6,520	6,520	100.00	165	165	100.00
1879–80	2,137	539	25.22	3,161	3,161	100.00	4,496	4,496	100.00	756	756	100.00
1880–1	581	235	40.45	3,342	3,342	100.00	4,416	4,416	100.00	513	513	100.00
1881–2	–	–	–	2,591	2,591	100.00	3,168	3,168	100.00	–	–	–
1882–3	1,574	994	63.15	1,963	1,963	100.00	2,984	2,974	99.66	398	398	100.00
1883–4	4,307	2,534	58.83	2,661	2,661	100.00	2,731	2,731	100.00	–	–	–
1884–5	4,109	2,016	49.06	2,191	2,191	100.00	6,304	5,827	92.43	601	601	100.00
1885–6	1,012	N.A.	–	1,656	1,656	100.00	4,771	3,688	77.30	–	–	–
1886–7	110	N.A.	–	2,291	2,291	100.00	3,916	2,857	72.96	–	–	–
1887–8	604	N.A.	–	2,130	2,130	100.00	2,777	3,836	–	–	–	–
1888–9	4,544	2,000	44.01	2,270	2,270	100.00	3,572	3,572	100.00	590	N.A.	–
1889–90	3,039	N.A.	–	2,897	2,897	100.00	3,426	3,426	100.00	–	–	–
1890–1	989	N.A.	–	3,435	N.A.	–	5,218	N.A.	–	1,087	N.A.	–
1891–2	–	–	–	3,285	N.A.	–	5,231	N.A.	–	1,060	N.A.	–
1892–3	–	–	–	2,620	N.A.	–	4,723	N.A.	–	–	–	–
1893–4	485	370	76.29	1,926	1,926	100.00	5,883	5,262	89.44	486	486	100.00
1894–5	1,029	486	47.23	3,185	3,185	100.00	7,200	7,277	–	711	711	100.00
1895–6	1,746	1,022	58.53	2,177	2,177	100.00	1,908	2,452	–	470	470	100.00
1896–7	802	560	69.83	3,043	3,043	100.00	2,417	2,417	100.00	–	–	–
1897–8	426	303	71.13	1,851	1,851	100.00	1,194	1,194	100.00	–	–	–

(Contd.)

Appendix I (contd.)

Year	Mauritius			Trinidad			Demerara			Jamaica		
	Total Emigration	Through Calcutta Port	Percentage to Total	Total Emigration	Through Calcutta Port	Percentage to Total	Total Emigration	Through Calcutta Port	Percentage to Total	Total Emigration	Through Calcutta Port	Percentage to Total
1898–9	—	—	—	1,258	1,258	100.00	2,380	2,380	100.00	623	N.A.	—
1899–1900	—	—	—	1,798	N.A.	—	4,959	N.A.	—	670	N.A.	—
1900–1	3,229	N.A.	—	2,450	N.A.	—	6,932	N.A.	—	—	—	—
TOTAL	4,17,329	2,43,447		99,332	95,305		2,13,597	1,73,575				

Source: For emigration through Calcutta Port:

(1) Grierson (1883), Appendix A.
(2) Proceedings of General Department—Annual Report, Appendix A for respective years. For total emigration to Four Sugar Colonies.
(3) Ferenzi Imre (1929), Table IV , pp. 904–5.

*Discrepancy exists in between total emigrants and emigrants through Calcutta Port
N.A.: Not available.

APPENDIX II–A

Annual Return of Emigrants by Age Despatched to Mauritius through
Calcutta Port during the Period 1875–6 to 1899–1900

Year	Under 10 years	From 10 to 20 years	From 20 to 30 years	From 30 to 40 years	Above 40 years	Total
1875–6	88	129	393	123	6	739
1876–7	–	–	–	–	–	–
1877–8	419	374	882	624	37	2,336
1878–9	291	143	420	337	29	1,220
1879–80	104	83	204	134	14	539
1880–1	44	51	102	33	5	235
1881–2	–	–	–	–	–	–
1882–3	134	205	528	117	10	994
1883–4	328	483	1,325	355	43	2,534
1884–5	270	355	1,050	307	34	2,016
1885–6	–	–	–	–	–	–
1886–7	–	–	–	–	–	–
1887–8	–	–	–	–	–	–
1888–9	–	–	–	–	–	–
1889–90	265	222	1,124	350	39	2,000
1890–1	–	–	–	–	–	–
1891–2	–	–	–	–	–	–
1892–3	–	–	–	–	–	–
1893–4	40	59	244	27	–	370
1894–5	36	32	384	32	2	486
1895–6	116	96	764	46	–	1,022
1896–7	27	55	454	24	–	560
1897–8	22	13	239	29	–	303
1898–9	–	–	–	–	–	–
1899–1900	–	–	–	–	–	–

Source: Computed from Proceedings. General Department, Annual Report, 1875–6 to 1899–1900.

APPENDIX II–B

Annual Return of Emigrants by Age Despatched to Demerara through Calcutta Port during the Period 1875–6 to 1899–1900

Year	Under 10 years	From 10 to 20 years	From 20 to 30 years	From 30 to 40 years	Above 40 years	Total
1875–6	455	696	2,395	288	15	3,849
1876–7	–	–	–	–	–	–
1877–8	1,891	1,335	4,522	525	15	8,288
1878–9	895	1,052	4,307	247	19	6,520
1879–80	542	976	2,772	188	18	4,496
1880–1	429	1,174	2,669	113	31	4,416
1881–2	312	754	1,953	129	20	3,168
1882–3	319	652	1,828	149	36	2,984
1883–4	292	593	1,659	163	24	2,731
1884–5	833	1,173	3,395	400	26	5,827
1885–6	508	686	2,282	208	4	3,688
1886–7	373	760	1,478	229	17	2,857
1887–8	479	965	2,176	213	3	3,836
1888–9	526	462	2,147	415	22	3,572
1889–90	517	317	2,177	405	10	3,426
1890–1	–	–	–	–	–	–
1891–2	–	–	–	–	–	–
1892–3	–	–	–	–	–	–
1893–4	605	575	3,791	285	6	5,262
1894–5	988	867	5,076	335	11	7,277
1895–6	339	252	1,767	90	4	2,452
1896–7	334	281	1,721	80	1	2,417
1897–8	89	96	983	25	1	1,194
1898–9	157	305	1,815	98	5	2,380
1899–1900	–	–	–	–	–	–

Source: Computed from Proceedings. General Department, Annual Report, 1875–6 to 1899–1900.

APPENDIX II–C

Annual Return of Emigrants by Age Despatched to Trinidad through Calcutta Port during the Period 1875–6 to 1899–1900

Year	Under 10 years	From 10 to 20 years	From 20 to 30 years	From 30 to 40 years	Above 40 years	Total
1875–6	255	392	886	141	9	1,653
1876–7	–	–	–	–	–	–
1877–8	321	553	1,135	119	23	2,151
1878–9	372	518	1,642	95	5	2,632
1879–80	446	706	1,885	118	6	3,161
1880–1	399	855	2,004	80	8	3,342
1881–2	290	722	1,526	51	2	2,591
1882–3	199	548	1,157	56	3	1,963
1883–4	290	647	1,594	123	7	2,661
1884–5	398	435	1,160	173	27	2,191
1885–6	255	264	994	140	3	1,656
1886–7	309	492	1,224	166	10	2,201
1887–8	330	507	1,150	137	6	2,130
1888–9	421	151	1,449	242	7	2,270
1889–90	530	276	1,640	418	33	2,897
1890–91	–	–	–	–	–	–
1891–2	–	–	–	–	–	–
1892–3	–	–	–	–	–	–
1893–4	238	188	1,334	162	4	1,926
1894–5	495	433	2,043	205	9	3,185
1895–6	368	217	1,540	52	–	2,177
1896–7	403	384	2,178	75	3	3,043
1897–8	102	163	1,527	58	1	1,851
1898–9	85	139	1,005	39	–	1,268
1899–1900	–	–	–	–	–	–

Source: Computed from Proceedings. General Department. Annual Report, 1875–6 to 1899–1900.

APPENDIX II–D

Annual Return of Emigrants by Age Despatched to Jamaica through
Calcutta Port during the Period 1875–6 to 1899–1900

Year	Under 10 years	From 10 to 20 years	From 20 to 30 years	From 30 to 40 years	Above 40 years	Total
1875–6	102	215	431	27	2	767
1876–7	–	–	–	–	–	–
1877–8	201	176	479	38	2	896
1878–9	22	50	90	3	–	165
1879–80	102	189	442	22	1	756
1880–1	57	127	325	4	–	513
1881–2	–	–	–	–	–	–
1882–3	32	124	237	5	–	398
1883–4	–	–	–	–	–	–
1884–5	97	106	349	45	4	601
1885–6	–	–	–	–	–	–
1886–7	–	–	–	–	–	–
1887–8	–	–	–	–	–	–
1888–9	–	–	–	–	–	–
1889–90	–	–	–	–	–	–
1890–1	–	–	–	–	–	–
1891–2	–	–	–	–	–	–
1892–3	–	–	–	–	–	–
1893–4	33	40	373	40	–	486
1894–5	74	82	496	59	–	711
1895–6	48	42	356	24	–	470
1896–7	–	–	–	–	–	–
1897–8	–	–	–	–	–	–
1898–9	–	–	–	–	–	–
1899–1900	–	–	–	–	–	–

Source: Computed from Proceedings. General Department, Annual Report, 1875–6 to 1899–1900.

APPENDIX III-A

Statement Showing Sex Ratio* of Emigrants Despatched through Calcutta Port to Four Sugar Colonies during 1842–70

Year	Emigrant despatched to			
	Demerara	Trinidad	Jamaica	Mauritius
1842	–	–	–	120
1843	–	–	–	133
1844	–	–	–	171
1845	176	180	169	198
1846	217	188	184	256
1847	131	144	129	118
1848	111	112	–	128
1849	–	–	–	144
1850	–	–	–	140
1851	134	146	–	164
1852	201	150	–	266
1853	213	210	–	158
1854	187	158	–	149
1855	383	320	–	257
1856	326	417	–	380
1857	681	660	–	461
1858	354	399	–	358
1859	397	312	398	297
1860	520	305	418	458
1861	255	221	268	244
1862	245	243	–	180
1863	243	225	–	271
1864	239	239	–	251
1865	329	373	–	292
1866	437	471	450	`415
1867	293	432	–	428
1868	381	425	399	372
1869	482	573	416	403
1870	345	363	363	402

Source: Computed from Geogeghan, pp. 77–81.
*Excluding children

APPENDIX III-B

Statement showing Sex Ratio of Emigrants Despatched through Calcutta Port to Four Sugar Colonies during 1877–8 to 1899–1900

Year	Emigrant despatched to			
	Demerara	Trinidad	Jamaica	Mauritius
1877–8	521	466	488	455
1878–9	456	442	514	593
1879–80	447	443	437	544
1880–1	422	441	438	577
1881–2	430	424	–	–
1882–3	434	429	401	504
1883–4	428	446	–	440
1884–5	470	510	473	453
1885–6	518	450	–	–
1886–7	452	462	–	–
1887–8	448	467	–	–
1888–9	465	479	–	–
1889–1890	458	471	–	385
1890–1	–	–	–	–
1891–2	–	–	–	–
1892–3	–	–	–	–
1893–4	450	488	434	386
1894–5	446	509	428	361
1895–6	469	601	446	368
1896–7	536	542	–	349
1897–8	474	530	–	335
1898–9	488	459	–	–
1899–1900	–	–	–	–

Source: Computed from Proceedings. General Department, Annual Report, 1877–8 to 1898.

APPENDIX IV-A

Annual Return of Emigrants Despatched to Mauritius through Calcutta Port Distributed by Caste and Religion for the Years 1877–8 to 1899–1900

Year	Hindoos						Mussalmans	Christians
	Total number of Emigrants	Brahmin/ higher caste	Agricul- turists	Artizans	Low Caste	Hindoos Total		
1877–8	2,336	298	589	101	1,055	2,043	292	1
1878–9	1,220	103	389	31	562	1,085	135	–
1879–80	539	79	171	37	148	435	104	–
1880–1	235	48	62	10	90	210	25	–
1881–2	–	–	–	–	–	–	–	–
1882–3	994	156	280	63	318	817	177	–
1883–4	2,534	431	709	103	856	2,099	434	–
1884–5	2,016	355	483	292	594	1,724	292	–
1885–6	–	–	–	–	–	–	–	–
1886–7	–	–	–	–	–	–	–	–
1887–8	–	–	–	–	–	–	–	–
1888–9	–	–	–	–	–	–	–	–
1889–90	2,000	220	636	210	683	1,749	246	5
1890–1	–	–	–	–	–	–	–	–
1891–2	–	–	–	–	–	–	–	–
1892–3	–	–	–	–	–	–	–	–
1893–4	370	36	170	44	90	340	30	–
1894–5	486	77	229	28	95	429	57	–
1895–6	1,022	147	467	60	324	998	24	–
1896–7	560	70	251	36	200	557	3	–
1897–8	303	15	115	28	143	301	2	–
1898–9	–	–	–	–	–	–	–	–
1899–1900	–	–	–	–	–	–	–	–

Source: Computed from Proceedings. General Department, Annual Report, 1877–8 to 1897–8.

APPENDIX IV-B

Annual Return of Emigrants Despatched through Calcutta Port to Demerara Distributed by Caste and Religion for the Years 1877–8 to 1899–1900

Year	Hindoos						Mussalmans	Christians
	Total number of Emigrants	Brahmin/ higher caste	Agricul- turists	Artizans	Low caste	Hindoos Total		
1877–8	8,288	786	1,853	288	4,425	7,352	931	5
1878–9	6,520	670	2,246	361	2,145	5,422	1,098	–
1879–80	8,014	741	1,122	231	1,424	3,518	964	14
1880–1	4,416	746	1,025	195	1,487	3,453	961	2
1881–2	3,168	589	787	151	950	2,477	689	2
1882–3	2,984	611	731	109	986	2,437	524	23
1883–4	2,731	487	718	136	963	2,304	426	1
1884–5	5,827	834	1,209	893	2,115	5,051	774	2
1885–6	3,688	444	655	768	1,340	3,207	477	4
1886–7	2,857	454	489	675	835	2,453	403	1
1887–8	3,836	724	615	843	1,089	3,271	563	2
1888–9	3,572	575	971	294	1,305	3,145	427	–
1889–90	3,426	421	1,037	275	1,299	3,032	393	1
1890–1	–	–	–	–	–	–	–	–
1891–2	–	–	–	–	–	–	–	–
1892–3	–	–	–	–	–	–	–	–
1893–4	5,262	414	2,396	361	1,259	4,430	831	1
1894–5	7,277	582	3,149	422	2,095	6,248	1,028	1
1895–6	2,452	148	944	152	951	2,195	255	2
1896–7	2,417	82	1,000	127	921	2,130	287	–
1897–8	1,194	9	475	71	516	1,071	123	–
1898–9	2,380	103	1,189	177	486	1,955	425	–
1899–1900	–	–	–	–	–	–	–	–

Source: Computed from Proceedings. General Department, Annual Report, 1877–8 to 1897–8.

APPENDIX IV-C

Annual Return of Emigrants Despatched through Calcutta Port to Trinidad
Distributed by Caste and Religion for the Years 1877–8 to 1899–1900

Year	Hindoos						Mussalmans	Christians
	Total number of Emigrants	Brahmin/ higher caste	Agricul- turists	Artizans	Low caste	Hindoos Total		
1877–8	2,151	307	561	101	878	1,847	304	–
1878–9	2,632	241	896	51	1,241	2,429	320	–
1879–80	3,161	485	939	154	921	2,499	658	4
1880–1	3,342	529	952	142	1,122	2,745	596	1
1881–2	2,591	475	665	98	899	2,137	454	–
1882–3	1,963	430	523	87	536	1,576	382	5
1883–4	2,661	581	684	102	829	2,196	463	2
1884–5	2,191	247	394	293	809	1,743	348	–
1885–6	1,656	236	253	350	584	1,423	232	1
1886–7	2,201	378	389	397	663	1,827	373	1
1887–8	2,130	342	380	369	753	1,844	286	–
1888–9	2,270	310	627	135	953	2,025	243	2
1889–90	2,897	313	810	230	1,207	2,560	330	7
1890–1	–	–	–	–	–	–	–	–
1891–2	–	–	–	–	–	–	–	–
1892–3	–	–	–	–	–	–	–	–
1893–4	1,926	312	691	131	549	1,683	242	1
1894–5	3,185	428	1,164	173	1,030	2,795	384	6
1895–6	2,177	179	783	102	976	2,040	137	–
1896–7	3,043	229	1,260	200	1,116	2,805	238	–
1897–8	1,851	103	824	94	708	1,729	122	–
1898–9	1,268	209	518	87	277	1,091	177	–
1899–1900	–	–	–	–	–	–	–	–

Source: Computed from Proceedings. General Department, Annual Report, 1877–8 to 1898–9.

APPENDIX IV-D

Annual Return of Emigrants Despatched through Calcutta Port to Jamaica Distributed by Caste and Religion for the Years 1877–8 to 1899–1900

Year			Hindoos				Mussalmans	Christians
	Total number of Emigrants	Brahmin/ higher caste	Agricul- turists	Artizans	Low caste	Hindoos Total		
1877–8	896	127	262	23	408	820	76	–
1878–9	165	21	61	3	55	140	25	–
1879–80	756	80	183	37	256	556	200	–
1880–1	513	102	126	16	192	436	77	–
1881–2	–	–	–	–	–	–	–	–
1882–3	398	114	74	19	101	308	87	3
1883–4	–	–	–	–	–	–	–	–
1884–5	601	89	114	94	215	512	89	–
1885–6	–	–	–	–	–	–	–	–
1886–7	–	–	–	–	–	–	–	–
1887–8	–	–	–	–	–	–	–	–
1888–9	–	–	–	–	–	–	–	–
1889–90	–	–	–	–	–	–	–	–
1890–1	–	–	–	–	–	–	–	–
1891–2	–	–	–	–	–	–	–	–
1892–3	–	–	–	–	–	–	–	–
1893–4	486	77	193	36	115	421	65	–
1894–5	711	98	317	40	177	632	79	–
1895–6	470	61	178	38	164	441	29	–
1896–7	–	–	–	–	–	–	–	–
1897–8	–	–	–	–	–	–	–	–
1898–9	–	–	–	–	–	–	–	–
1899–1900	–	–	–	–	–	–	–	–

Source: Computed from Proceedings. General Department, Annual Report, 1877–8 to 1895–6.

APPENDIX V-A

Places whence Emigrants Came to Calcutta for Embarkation to
Mauritius during the Period 1874–5 to 1899–1900

Year	Emigrants came from					
	Bengal	Behar	NWPs	Oudh	Other Places	Total
1874–5	242	2,295	1,962	350	65	4,914
1875–6	22	239	290	137	51	739
1876–7	–	–	–	–	–	–
1877–8	84	907	1,221	90	34	2,336
1878–9	37	498	643	29	13	1,220
1879–80	24	245	221	24	25	539
1880–1	36	103	82	11	3	235
1881–2	–	–	–	–	–	–
1882–3	73	404	371	127	19	994
1883–4	139	980	859	275	281	2,534
1884–5	81	814	665	129	327	2,016
1885–6	–	–	–	–	–	–
1886–7	–	–	–	–	–	–
1887–8	–	–	–	–	–	–
1888–9	–	–	–	–	–	–
1889–90	54	860	823	222	41	2,000
1890–1	–	–	–	–	–	–
1891–2	–	–	–	–	–	–
1892–3	–	–	–	–	–	–
1893–4	16	93	178	77	6	370
1894–5	11	98	190	158	29	486
1895–6	–	68	526	415	13	1,022
1896–7	–	31	325	189	15	560
1897–8	–	1	163	134	5	303
1898–9	–	–	–	–	–	–
1899–1900	–	–	–	–	–	–

Source: Computed from Proceedings. General Department, Annual Report, 1874–5 to 1897–8.

APPENDIX V-B

Places whence Emigrants Came to Calcutta for Embarkation to
Demerara during the Period 1874–5 to 1899–1900

Year	Emigrants came from					
	Bengal	Behar	NWPs	Oudh	Other Places	Total
1874–5	119	1,049	2,129	601	44	3,942
1875–6	147	1,039	1,741	810	112	3,849
1876–7	–	–	–	–	–	–
1877–8	42	510	4,581	2,118	1,037	8,288
1878–9	74	639	3,671	2,065	121	6,520
1879–80	121	583	2,712	634	396	4,496
1880–1	76	507	2,801	598	434	4,416
1881–2	54	341	1,888	465	420	3,168
1882–3	63	597	1,324	454	546	2,984
1883–4	3	640	1,322	454	301	2,731
1884–5	697	2,109	2,002	784	234	5,827
1885–6	203	1,597	1,273	531	84	3,688
1886–7	149	946	1,216	453	93	2,857
1887–8	40	870	1,939	878	109	3,836
1888–9	27	930	1,868	675	70	3,572
1889–90	23	641	1,872	818	72	3,426
1890–1	–	–	–	–	–	–
1891–2	–	–	–	–	–	–
1892–3	–	–	–	–	–	–
1893–4	76	835	2,647	1,451	253	5,262
1894–5	59	874	3,821	2,255	268	7,277
1895–6	8	202	1,433	774	35	2,452
1896–7	8	145	1,548	685	31	2,417
1897–8	2	132	742	304	14	1,194
1898–9	15	212	1,111	946	96	2,380
1899–1900	–	–	–	–	–	–

Source: Computed from Proceedings. General Department, Annual Report, 1874–5 to 1898– 9.

APPENDIX V-C

Places whence Emigrants came to Calcutta for Embarkation to Trinidad
during the Period 1874–5 to 1899–1900

Year	Emigrants came from					
	Bengal	Behar	NWPs	Oudh	Other places	Total
1874–5	252	308	1,610	320	50	2,540
1875–6	98	281	967	258	49	1,653
1876–7	–	–	–	–	–	–
1877–8	32	293	1,273	1,000	34	2,632
1878–9	103	298	1,001	578	171	2,151
1879–80	75	572	1,576	820	118	3,161
1880–1	25	319	1,976	882	140	3,342
1881–2	16	959	1,375	736	360	2,591
1882–3	10	98	1,022	663	170	1,963
1883–4	50	461	1,086	624	440	2,661
1884–5	134	1,027	731	199	100	2,191
1885–6	46	859	460	256	35	1,656
1886–7	57	723	890	429	102	2,201
1887–8	19	442	1,101	481	87	2,130
1888–9	19	621	1,214	336	80	2,270
1889–90	52	812	1,530	448	55	2,897
1890–1	–	–	–	–	–	–
1891–2	–	–	–	–	–	–
1892–3	–	–	–	–	–	–
1893–4	76	462	1,001	319	68	1,926
1894–5	12	648	1,840	609	76	3,185
1895–6	–	100	1,440	614	23	2,177
1896–7	1	296	1,916	783	47	3,043
1897–8	8	172	1,088	510	73	1,851
1898–9	3	77	749	394	45	1,268
1899–1900	–	–	–	–	–	–

Source: Computed from Proceedings. General Department, Annual Report, 1874–5 to 1898–9.

APPENDIX V-D

Places whence Emigrants came to Calcutta for Embarkation to Jamaica during the Period 1874–5 to 1899–1900

Year	Emigrants came from					
	Bengal	Behar	NWPs	Oudh	Other places	Total
1874–5	27	411	641	155	24	1,258
1875–6	5	92	400	245	25	767
1876–7	–	–	–	–	–	–
1877–8	–	–	–	–	–	–
1878–9	–	6	46	110	3	165
1879–80	13	95	560	70	18	756
1880–1	–	8	348	106	51	513
1881–2	–	–	–	–	–	–
1882–3	–	9	205	113	71	398
1883–4	–	–	–	–	–	–
1884–5	24	287	199	77	14	601
1885–6	–	–	–	–	–	–
1886–7	–	–	–	–	–	–
1887–8	–	–	–	–	–	–
1888–9	–	–	–	–	–	–
1889–90	–	–	–	–	–	–
1890–1	–	–	–	–	–	–
1891–2	–	–	–	–	–	–
1892–3	–	–	–	–	–	–
1893–4	32	185	154	92	23	486
1894–5	9	126	337	233	6	711
1895–6	–	24	253	185	8	470
1896–7	–	–	–	–	–	–
1897–8	–	–	–	–	–	–
1898–9	–	–	–	–	–	–
1899–1900	–	–	–	–	–	–

Source: Computed from Proceedings. General Department, Annual Report, 1874–5 to 1895–6.

Statement Showing the Number of East Indian Emigrants who have Returned Calcutta from the Four Sugar Colonies with the Amount of their Savings, Remittance, etc., during the Period 1872–3 to 1899–1900

Year	Mauritius — No. of souls returned	Mauritius — Savings Rs.	A.	P.	Mauritius — Average Rs.	A.	P.	Mauritius — No. of souls returned	Mauritius — Savings Rs.	A.	P.	Mauritius — Average Rs.	A.	P.	Demerara — No. of souls returned	Demerara — Savings Rs.	A.	P.	Demerara — Average Rs.	A.	P.	Jamaica — No. of souls returned	Jamaica — Savings Rs.	A.	P.	Jamaica — Average Rs.	A.	P.
1872–3	74	42,774	0	0	578	0	—	—	—	—	—	—	—	—	876	2,16,106	8	8	246	—	—	—	—	—	—	—	—	—
1873–4	—	—	—	—	—	—	—	—	—	—	—	—	—	—	—	—	—	—	—	—	—	—	—	—	—	—	—	—
1874–5	1,837	1,81,266	0	0	98	—	—	405	1,06,635	14	0	263	—	—	801	1,63,291	2	4	203	—	—	—	—	—	—	—	—	—
1875–6	—	—	—	—	—	—	—	—	—	—	—	—	—	—	—	—	—	—	—	—	—	—	—	—	—	—	—	—
1876–7	1,782	2,86,989	0	0	161	0	3	2	5,687	8	0	2,843	12	0	443	93,442	3	0	210	14	10	268	20,272	0	0	75	10	3
1877–8	1,284	1,92,090	0	0	149	—	—	459	1,26,626	7	3	275	—	—	489	1,01,861	6	8	208	—	—	307	52,349	0	4	—	—	—
1878–9	1,402	2,37,567	0	0	169	—	—	—	—	—	—	—	—	—	1,599	3,88,949	15	10	243	—	—	227	25,217	0	0	—	—	—
1879–80	1,602	2,76,538	0	0	172	—	—	473	1,23,557	9	0	261	—	—	1,118	2,47,691	7	2	221	—	—	407	47,811	0	0	—	—	—
1880–1	1,502	2,01,545	0	0	134	—	—	446	1,42,916	0	0	320	—	—	1,566	3,03,620	7	10	193	—	—	361	58,194	11	8	—	—	—
1881–2	849	1,35,489	0	0	159	—	—	456	1,28,125	3	1	280	—	—	970	2,22,882	15	0	459	—	—	399	88,182	12	9	—	—	—
1882–3	1,206	1,36,394	0	0	113	—	—	—	—	—	—	—	—	—	1,501	3,54,898	9	1	236	—	—	442	48,591	0	0	—	—	—
1883–4	1,311	1,88,941	0	0	144	1	10	497	1,58,725	8	3	319	5	10	1,468	3,87,290	12	7	263	13	0	404	67,329	0	0	166	10	5
1884–5	1,052	1,91,943	0	0	181	8	0	678	2,42,102	6	9	357	1	4	1,569	3,91,514	6	3	249	8	5	78	17,966	7	4	230	5	5
1885–6	1,472	62,758	0	0	42	10	2	—	—	—	—	—	—	—	583	1,48,443	5	2	254	9	11	475	91,019	2	11	191	7	9
1886–7	1,196	31,334	0	0	26	3	2	620	1,35,608	12	5	220	13	9	1,895	2,90,200	0	0	154	9	8	—	—	—	—	—	—	—
1887–8	1,181	43,650	0	0	36	15	4	546	1,52,402	11	10	279	2	0	1,844	2,46,476	8	8	133	10	7	161	38,471	1	9	238	15	2
1888–9	464	22,008	0	0	47	6	10	678	1,60,875	0	0	237	4	5	1,389	1,97,084	8	9	141	14	4	555	93,864	8	5	169	6	10
1889–90	612	35,941	0	0	58	11	7	436	1,12,871	12	2	258	14	1	2,011	2,49,865	3	0	124	3	11	—	—	—	—	—	—	—
1890–1	—	—	—	—	—	—	—	—	—	—	—	—	—	—	—	—	—	—	—	—	—	—	—	—	—	—	—	—
1891–2	—	—	—	—	—	—	—	—	—	—	—	—	—	—	—	—	—	—	—	—	—	—	—	—	—	—	—	—

(Contd.)

Appendix VI (contd.)

Year	Mauritius													Demerara							Jamaica						
	No. of souls returned	Savings with the returned migrants			Average amount of savings			No. of souls returned	Savings with the returned migrants			Average amount of savings			No. of souls returned	Savings with the returned migrants			Average amount of savings			No. of souls returned	Savings with the returned migrants			Savings with the returned migrants		
		Rs.	A.	P.	Rs.	A.	P.		Rs.	A.	P.	Rs.	A.	P.		Rs.	A.	P.	Rs.	A.	P.		Rs.	A.	P.	Rs.	A.	P.
1892–3	–	–	–	–	–	–	–	–	–	–	–	–	–	–	–	–	–	–	–	–	–	–	–	–	–	–	–	–
1893–4	708	11,945	0	0	16	13	11	697	1,33,307	1	6	191	5	1	202	3,63,571	10	7	180	11	2	373	25,063	14	3	67	3	1
1894–5	254	6,375	0	0	25	1	6	740	1,43,013	11	11	193	4	2	1,214	2,32,613	7	9	191	9	8	–	–	–	–	–	–	–
1895–6	391	8,178	0	0	20	14	7	950	2,42,134	0	2	254	5	5	2,774	5,80,404	1	5	209	3	8	348	56,056	0	10	161	1	3
1896–7	394	13,959	0	0	35	6	10	700	1,56,901	5	4	224	2	3	1,345	2,45,482	15	5	182	8	3	–	–	–	–	–	–	–
1897–8	368	8,725	0	0	23	11	4	713	1,51,740	3	0	212	13	1	2,608	2,83,823	1	5	108	13	2	–	–	–	–	–	–	–
1898–9	433	6,451	0	0	14	14	4	747	1,06,061	11	10	141	15	8	1,558	2,14,403	4	2	137	9	9	–	–	–	–	–	–	–
1899–	–	–	–	–	–	–	–	–	–	–	–	–	–	–	–	–	–	–	–	–	–	–	–	–	–	–	–	–
1900																												

*Amount deposited in the colonial bank for remittance 551 return emigrants.

Source: Computed from Proceedings of the General Department Annual Report on Emigration from the port of Calcutta to British and foreign colonies for the respective years. Section IV. Disembarkation.

Note: Average amount of savings for the years 1872–3, 1874–5 and 1877–8 to 1882–3 has been rounded to rupees only.

APPENDIX VII-A

Statement Showing the Number of Emigrants Previously
Returned from Mauritius and Re-emigrated to the Various Colonies during
the period 1877–8 to 1889–90 and 1893–4

Year	No. of souls returned	Total number of return emigrants who re-emigrated	Colonies where re-emigrated emigrants proceeded				
			Mauritius	*Jamaica*	*Demerara*	*Trinidad*	*Other places*
1877–8	1,284	121	102	6	8	4	1
1878–9	1,402	120	48	1	35	8	18
1879–80	1,602	118	53	1	28	17	19
1880–1	1,502	50	–	2	19	7	22
1881–2	849	–	–	–	–	–	–
1882–3	1,206	206	118	20	36	4	28
1883–4	1,311	203	195	–	4	4	–
1884–5	1,052	198	158	1	36	3	–
1885–6	1,472	31	–	–	18	13	–
1886–7	1,196	51	–	–	24	27	–
1887–8	1,181	30	–	–	18	12	–
1888–9	464	45	–	–	23	22	–
1889–90	612	37	16	–	12	9	–
1893–4	708	–	–	–	–	–	–

Source: Computed from Proceedings General Department Annual Report, 1877–8 to 1889–90 and 1893–4.

Note: Figures related to Calcutta Port only.

APPENDIX VII-B

Statement Showing the Number of Emigrants Previously Returned
from Demerara and Re–emigrated to the Various Colonies during
the Period 1877–8 to 1893–4

Year	No. of souls returned	Total number of return emigrants who re-emigrated	Colonies where re-emigrated emigrants proceeded				
			Mauritius	Jamaica	Demerara	Trinidad	Other places
1877–8	489	99	19	6	66	3	5
1878–9	1,599	217	2	1	191	10	13
1879–80	1,118	205	3	–	164	25	13
1880–1	1,566	245	44	–	168	18	15
1881–2	970	208	21	16	140	23	8
1882–3	1,501	320	8	41	220	14	37
1883–4	1,468	236	27	–	173	36	–
1884–5	1,569	322	23	8	265	26	–
1885–6	583	205	–	–	183	22	–
1886–7	1,895	297	–	–	266	31	–
1887–8	1,844	238	–	–	192	46	–
1888–9	1,389	285	–	–	205	80	–
1889–90	2,011	222	4	–	162	56	–
1893–4	202	–	–	–	–	–	–

Source: Computed from proceedings General Department Annual Report, 1877–8 to 1889–90
and 1893–4.

Note: Figures related to Calcutta Port only.

APPENDIX VII-C

Statement Showing the Number of Emigrants Previously
Returned from Trinidad and Re–emigrated to the Various Colonies
during the Period 1877–8 to 1889–90 and 1893–4

Year	No. of souls returned	Total number of return emigrants who re-emigrated	Colonies where re-emigrated emigrants proceeded				
			Mauritius	Jamaica	Demerara	Trinidad	Other places
1877–8	459	40	7	3	5	19	6
1878–9	–	82	–	–	6	66	10
1879–80	473	92	2	1	10	75	4
1880–1	446	35	–	–	4	31	–
1881–2	456	17	1	1	15	–	–
1882–3	–	129	10	29	29	33	28
1883–4	497	22	3	–	4	15	–
1884–5	678	74	6	1	13	54	–
1885–6	–	42	–	–	14	28	–
1886–7	620	112	–	–	27	85	–
1887–8	546	63	–	–	23	40	–
1888–9	678	106	–	–	32	74	–
1889–90	436	70	–	–	21	49	–
1893–4	697	–	–	–	–	–	–

Source: Computed from Proceedings General Department Annual Report, 1877–8 to 1889–90
and 1893–4.

Note: Figures related to Calcutta port only.

APPENDIX VII-D

Statement Showing the Number of Emigrants Previously Returned
from Jamaica and Re–emigrated to the Various Colonies during
the Period 1877–8 to 1889–90 and 1893–4

Year	No. of souls returned	Total number of return emigrants who re-emigrated	Colonies where re-emigrated emigrants proceeded				
			Mauritius	Jamaica	Demerara	Trinidad	Other places
1877–8	307	10	2	7	–	1	–
1878–9	227	49	1	11	21	6	10
1879–80	407	89	4	2	61	18	4
1880–1	361	60	–	3	37	12	8
1881–2	399	–	–	–	–	–	–
1882–3	442	3	1	2	–	–	–
1883–4	404	47	12	–	24	11	–
1884–5	78	36	3	4	17	9	–
1885–6	475	19	–	–	13	6	–
1886–7	–	52	–	–	27	25	–
1887–8	161	46	–	–	26	20	–
1888–9	555	29	–	–	25	4	–
1889–90	–	63	9	–	32	22	–
1893–4	373	–	–	–	–	–	–

Source: Computed from proceedings General Department Annual Report, 1877–8 to 1889–90 and 1893–4.

Note: Figures related to Calcutta Port only.

APPENDIX VIII

Statement of Mortality in Depots among Emigrants and Causes of Deaths during 1877–8 to 1889–90

Emigration Depots/Year	Number of Emigrants accommodated	Number of deaths	Percentage of Mortality	Causes of death						
				Diarrhoea	Dysentery	Cholera	Fever	Chest affections	Other diseases	Total
DEMERARA										
1877–8	9,668	60	0.62	9	6	6	6	7	26	60
1878–9	7,263	34	0.47	2	6	3	3	4	16	34
1879–80	4,851	2	0.04	–	1	–	–	1	–	2
1880–1	5,085	20	0.39	4	2	–	4	6	4	20
1881–2	3,642	17	0.47	4	1	–	4	6	2	17
1882–3	3,513	14	0.39	1	2	1	6	1	3	14
1883–4	3,296	18	0.55	–	1	–	9	1	7	18
1884–5	7,376	39	0.53	2	4	–	8	12	13	39
1885–6	5,150	58	1.13	1	4	2	39	12	–	58
1886–7	3,827	11	0.29	3	2	1	2	–	3	11
1887–8	4,553	26	0.57	4	4	2	3	8	5	26
1888–9	4,135	21	0.51	2	2	3	3	7	4	21
1889–90	4,261	44	1.03	–	–	–	–	–	–	–
TRINIDAD										
1877–8	2,821	6	0.21	–	1	3	–	1	1	6
1878–9	3,093	11	0.35	4	2	1	–	3	1	11
1879–80	3,602	13	0.36	2	–	1	5	2	3	13

(Contd.)

Appendix VIII (contd.)

Emigration Depots/Year	Number of Emigrants accommodated	Number of deaths	Percentage of Mortality	Causes of death						
				Diarrhoea	Dysentery	Cholera	Fever	Chest affections	Other diseases	Total
1880–1	3,982	33	0.83	5	13	1	2	7	5	33
1881–2	2,990	13	0.43	2	6	1	–	2	2	13
1882–3	2,402	22	0.92	3	3	1	6	6	3	22
1883–4	3,224	13	0.40	1	2	–	4	3	3	13
1884–5	3,377	73	2.16	4	7	1	15	1	45	73
1885–6	2,265	11	0.48	2	2	2	–	2	3	11
1886–7	2,664	3	0.11	–	1	–	–	1	1	3
1887–8	2,711	23	0.85	–	5	1	9	6	2	23
1888–9	3,045	20	0.66	–	4	–	7	5	4	20
1889–90	3,702	13	0.35	–	–	–	–	–	–	–
JAMAICA										
1877–7	1,156	9	0.78	–	3	1	–	5	–	9
1878–9	232	1	0.43	–	–	–	–	–	1	1
1879–80	1,024	10	0.97	–	2	6	–	2	–	10
1880–1	713	4	0.56	2	1	–	–	1	–	4
1881–2	–	–	–	–	–	–	–	–	–	–
1882–3	560	–	0.00	–	–	–	–	–	–	–
1883–4	–	–	–	–	–	–	–	–	–	–
1884–5	779	16	2.05	–	1	–	13	2	–	16
1885–6	–	–	–	–	–	–	–	–	–	–

(Contd.)

Appendix VIII (contd.)

Emigration Depots/Year	Number of Emigrants accommodated	Number of deaths	Percentage of Mortality	Causes of death						
				Diarrhoea	Dysentery	Cholera	Fever	Chest affections	Other diseases	Total
1886–7	–	–	–	–	–	–	–	–	–	–
1887–8	–	–	–	–	–	–	–	–	–	–
1888–9	–	–	–	–	–	–	–	–	–	–
1889–90	–	–	–	–	–	–	–	–	–	–
MAURITIUS										
1877–8	3,044	41	1.35	16	3	7	4	4	7	41
1878–9	1,316	8	0.61	–	1	2	2	1	2	8
1879–80	520	2	0.38	–	1	1	–	–	–	2
1880–1	302	1	0.31	–	–	–	–	–	1	1
1881–2	155	–	0.00	–	–	–	–	–	–	–
1882–3	1,518	13	0.86	1	4	2	2	1	3	13
1883–4	3,485	28	0.80	3	7	7	4	3	4	28
1884–5	2,566	24	0.93	1	3	3	6	6	5	24
1885–6	–	–	–	–	–	–	–	–	–	–
1886–7	–	–	–	–	–	–	–	–	–	–
1887–8	–	–	–	–	–	–	–	–	–	–
1888–9	–	–	–	–	–	–	–	–	–	–
1889–90	2,531	38	1.50	–	–	–	–	–	–	–

Source: Computed from Proceedings, General Department Annual Report, 1877–8 to 1889–90

APPENDIX IX

Statement Showing the Commencement and Resumption of Emigration to Four Sugar Colonies, in Regular System from India, 1842–1900

Year	Mauritius	Demerara	Trinidad	Jamaica	Remarks
1842	Commenced	None	None	None	Interruption to emigration
1843	......	......	......	......	have been due chiefly to the
1844	......	......	......	......	absence of requisitions from
					the colonies
1845	......	Commenced	Commenced	Commenced	High demand for
1846					labour to the sugar
1847					colonies
1848				Stopped	
1849	......	Stopped	Stopped	......	During 1849–50
1850	......	......	......	......	emigration was suspended
					in West Indies party due
					to high death rate on the
					long sea journey and partly
					also owing to the decline of
					the sugar industry
1851	......	Resumed	Resumed	......	
1852	......	......	......	......	
1853	......	......	......	......	
1854	......	......	......	......	
1855	......	......	......	......	
1856	......	......	......	......	Emigration to Mauritus
1857	......	......	......	......	temporarily declined due
1858	......	......	......	......	to the cause of frightful
					mortality among coolies and
					passing of an Act
					(XIX of 1956) related to
					protection of emigrants
1859	......	......	......	Resumed	
1860	......	......	......	......	
1861	......	......	......	......	
1862	......	......	......	Stopped	
1863	......	......	......	......	
1864	......	......	......	......	
1865	......	......	......	......	
1866	......	......	......	Resumed	
1867	......	......	......	Stopped	
1868	......	......	......	Resumed	
1869	......	......	......	......	
1870	......	......	......	Stopped	
1871	......	......	Stopped	......	
1872	......	......	......	......	
1873	......	......	......	......	
1874	......	......	......	......	
1875	......	......	......	......	

(Contd.)

Appendix IX (*contd.*)

Year	Mauritius	Demerara	Trinidad	Jamaica	Remarks
1876	......	......	......	Resumed	
1877	......	......	......	Stopped	
1878	......	......	Resumed	Resumed	Emigration to colonies, received a remarkable impulse
1879	......	......	......	......	
1880	......	......	......	......	
1881	Stopped	......	......	Stopped	Demerara was the largest
1882	Resumed	......	......	Resumed	coolie-imparting colony and has a thoroughly well-organized emigration service
1883	......	......	......	Stopped	
1884	......	......	......	Resumed	
1885	Stopped	......	......	Stopped	Decline in price of sugar, requisition were cancelled
1886	Resumed	......	......	......	
1887	......	......	......	......	
1888	......	......	......	Resumed	
1889	......	......	......	Stopped	
1890	......	......	......	Resumed	
1891	......	......	......	......	In the decade 1890–1900,
1892	Stopped	......	......	Stopped	plantation labour demand
1893	Resumed	......	......	Resumed	dwindled in Mauritius. But
1894	......	......	......	......	the case is not true for
1895	......	......	......	......	Demerara and Trinidad,
1896	......	......	......	Stopped	immigration continued on
1897	......	......	......	......	a modest scale there.
1898	Stopped	......	......	Resumed	Jamaica failed to be a good
1899	......	......	......	......	importer of coolies due to its
1900	Resumed	......	......	Stopped	large population and opposition to coolie immigration

Source: Computed from Grierson, 1883, p. 5 and Sources (2) and (3) of Table Appendix I.

Note: Emigration to Mauritius practically stopped during the period 1910–11. But this flow came to an end in Trinidad and Demerara during 1916–17 and in Jamaica in 1913–14 (The period of 1901–17 is beyond the scope of our study).

APPENDIX X

Proportion of Brahmin/Higher Caste to Total Emigrants from Calcutta Port to
the Four Sugar Colonies, Mauritius, Demerara, Trinidad and Jamaica
during the Period 1877–8 to 1898–9

Year	Proportion of Brahmin/higher caste to			
	Mauritius	Demerara	Trinidad	Jamaica
1877–8	14.6	10.7	16.6	15.5
1878–9	9.5	12.4	9.9	15.0
1879–80	18.2	21.1	19.4	14.4
1880–1	22.9	–	19.3	23.4
1881–2	–	23.8	22.2	–
1882–3	19.1	25.1	27.3	37.0
1883–4	20.5	21.1	26.5	17.4
1884–5	20.6	16.5	14.2	–
1885–6	–	13.8	16.7	–
1886–7	–	18.5	20.7	–
1887–8	–	22.1	18.4	–
1888–9	–	18.3	15.3	–
1889–90	12.6	13.9	12.2	–
1890–1	–	–	–	–
1891–2	–	–	–	–
1892–3	–	–	–	–
1893–4	10.6	9.3	18.5	18.3
1894–5	22.6	9.3	15.3	15.5
1895–6	14.7	6.7	8.8	13.8
1896–7	12.7	3.8	8.2	–
1897–8	5.0	–	6.0	–
1898–9	–	5.3	19.2	–

Source: Computed from Proceedings, General Department, Annual Report for the years 1877–8
to 1898–9.

Select Bibliography

Primary Sources

Archival Documents (West Bengal State Archives)

(i) Reports of the Government of Bengal

Government of Bengal, 'Annual Report on Emigration from the Port of Calcutta to British and Foreign Colonies for the years 1870–71', General Department, Emigration Branch, Calcutta: West Bengal State Archives (hereafter WBSA).

Government of Bengal, 'The Report of the Protector of Emigrants to British and Foreign Colonies during the year ending 31st March 1878', Resolution, General Department, Emigration Branch, Calcutta: WBSA, September 1878.

Government of Bengal, 'Annual Report on Emigration from the Port of Calcutta to British and Foreign Colonies', General Department Emigration Branch, Calcutta: WBSA for the years 1874–5 to 1889–90 and 1893–4 to 1898–9.

Grierson, George A. 'Report on Colonial Emigration from the Bengal Presidency', General Department, Emigration Branch, Appendix A, File 15–20/21, Government of Bengal, Calcutta: WBSA, June 1883.

Lubbock, Nevil, 'Present Position of the West Indian Colonies', Read at a meeting of the Royal Colonial Institute, London, Proceedings, Finance Department, Emigration Branch, File-72, Calcutta: WBSA, July 1877.

Muir-Mackenzie, J.W.P., 'Report on the Condition of Indian Immigrants in Mauritius', General Department, Emigration Branch, July 1895, Calcutta: WBSA, July 1895.

(ii) Correspondences of the Government of Bengal

Government of Bengal, General Department, General Branch, no. 21, 3 June 1852, Calcutta: WBSA.

Government of Bengal, General Department, General Branch, no. 27, 9 August 1855, Calcutta: WBSA.

Government of Bengal, General Department, Emigration Branch, June 1870–1, Calcutta: WBSA.

Government of Bengal, General Department, Emigration Branch, September 1873, Calcutta: WBSA.

Government of Bengal, General Department, Misc. Branch, November 1877, Calcutta: WBSA.

Government of Bengal, General Department, Emigration Branch, September 1878, Calcutta: WBSA.

Government of Bengal, 'On the subject of the revision of the system of emigration from India to British and Foreign Colonies', General Department, Emigration Branch, September 1879, Calcutta: WBSA.

Government of Bengal, General Department, Misc. Branch, September 1880, Calcutta: WBSA.

Government of Bengal, General Department, Emigration Branch, November 1881, Calcutta: WBSA.

Government of Bengal, General Department, Emigration Branch, December 1886, Calcutta: WBSA.

Government of Bengal, General Department, Emigration Branch, August 1887, Calcutta: WBSA.

Government of Bengal, General Department, Emigration Branch, August 1889, Calcutta: WBSA.

Government of Bengal, General Department, Emigration Branch, May 1890, Calcutta: WBSA.

Government of Bengal, General Department, Emigration Branch, November 1891, Calcutta: WBSA.

Government of Bengal, General Department, 1893, Calcutta: WBSA.

Public Documents

(i) Parliamentary Papers (PP)

Great Britain, Geoghegan, J., 'Note on Emigration from India', PP, vol. XLVII, 1874.

Great Britain, 'Emigration of Indian Labourers to the Mauritius', PP, vol. XXXV, 1844.

Great Britain, Sanderson Commission, 'Report of the Committee on Emigration from India to the Crown Colonies and Protectorates', PP, Great Britain, vol. XXII, 1910.

Great Britain, 'The Report of the Commissioners of Enquiry into the Condition and Treatment of Immigrants in British Guiana', PP, vol. XX, 1871.

(ii) Surveys, Reports and Gazetteers

Census of Mauritius and its dependencies taken on 6 April 1891, Mauritius. The Central Printing Establishment, 1892.

Ferenczi, Imre, *International Migrations: Statistics with Introduction and Notes*, vol. I, Geneva: ILO; New York: NBER, Inc., 1929.

Government of Bengal, *Report on the Condition of the Lower Classes of Population in Bengal*, Bengal Revenue Department, Calcutta: Bengal Secretariat Press, 1888.

Great Britain, Report of the Royal Commission in India, 1931, London, published by His Majesty's Stationary Office, 1931.

Government of India, Bengal Census, District Census Report, Shahabad District, 1891.

———, Census of Lower Provinces of Bengal, Provincial Table III, 1891.

Kuczynski, R.R., *Demographic Survey of the British Colonial Empire*, vol. II (issued under the auspices of the Royal Institute of International Affairs), London and New York: OUP, 1949.

———, Census of India, 1901, vol. VI, Appendix I, Migration Statement.

McNeil, James and Chimmanlal, *Report on the Condition of Indian Immigrants in the Four British Colonies: Trinidad, British Guiana or Demerara, Jamaica and Fiji and in the Dutch Colony of Surinam or Dutch Guiana*, Simla: Government Central Press (Government of India), 1914.

——— , Census of India, 1901, vol. VI, Appendix I, Migration Statement.

Nevill, H.R., *Gazetteers of the United Provinces of Agra and Oudh*, Allahabad, Ballia District, vol. XXX, Allahabad: Superintendent of Government Press, 1907.

———, *Gazetteer of the United Provinces of Agra and Oudh*, Benares District, vol. XXIV, Allahabad: Superintendent of Government Press, 1909.

———, *Gazetteer of the United Provinces of Agra and Oudh*, Ghazipur District, vol. XXI, Allahabad: Superintendent of Government Press, 1909.

———, *Gazetteer of the United Provinces of Agra and Oudh*, Gorakhpur District, vol. XXXI, Allahabad: Superintendent of Government Press, 1909.

Report of the Truth an Justice Commission, Mauritius, vol. I , 2011, printed by Government Printing (www.wip.org/files/defaut/files/ROL/TJC, vol. I.pdf.)

Secondary Sources

Books

Bhattacharya, Dhiresh, *A Concise History of the Indian Economy, 1750–1950*, 2nd edn., New Delhi: Prentice Hall of India, 1979.

Beachy, R.W., *The British West Indies: Sugar Industry in the Late 19th Century*, Oxford: Basil Blackwell, 1957.

Bissoondoyal, Basdeo, *The Truth about Mauritius*, Bombay: Bharatiya Vidya Bhavan, 1968.

Chattopadhyay, Haraprasad, *Internal Migration in India: A Case Study of Bengal*, Calcutta and New Delhi: K.P. Bagchi & Company, 1987.

Craton, Michael, *Testing the Chains, Resistance to Slavery in the British West Indies*, Ithaca, NY: Cornell University Press, 1982.

Cumpston, I.M., *Indians Overseas in British Territories, 1834–1854*, London: OUP, 1953.

Hazareesingh, K., *History of Indians in Mauritius*, London: Macmillan Education, 1975.

Hunter, W.W., *A Statistical Account of Bengal*, vol. XVIII, London: Trubner & Co., 1977.

Nwulia, Moses D.E., *The History of Slavery in Mauritius and the Seychelles, 1810–1875*, London: Associated University Press, 1981.

Nath, Dwarka, *History of Indians in British Guiana*, with a Foreword by Sir Gordon Lethem, Published with the authority of his Excellency the Governor of British Guiana, London, 1970.

Ramdin, Rom, *Arising from Bondage: A History of the Indo-Caribbean People*, London: I.B. Tauris Publishers, 2000.

Ridley, S., *Report on the Condition of Indians in Mauritius*, Manager, New Delhi: Government of India Press, 1940.

Saha, Panchanan, *Emigration of Indian Labour (1834–1900)*, New Delhi: People's Publishing House, 1970.

Temperley, Howard, *British Antislavery (1833–1870)*, London: Longman Group, 1972.

Tinker, Huge, *A New System of Slavery: The Export of Indian Labour Overseas, 1830–1920*, Institute of Race Relations, London and New York: OUP, 1974.

Tinker, Huge, *The Banyan Tree: Overseas Emigrants from India, Pakistan and Bangladesh*, Oxford: OUP, 1977.

Titmuss, Richard M. and Brian Abel-Smith, *Social Policies and Population Growth in Mauritius: Report to the Governor of Mauritius*, assisted by Tony Lynes, London: Methuen, 1960.

Journals

Carter, Marina and Crispin Bates, 'Empire and Locality: A Global Dimension to the 1857 Indian Uprising', *Journal of Global History*, vol. 5, 2010, pp. 51–73. © London School of Economics and Political Science, 2010. http//www.academia.edu/303586/Empire_and_Locality_a_Global_Dimension_to_the_1857_Indian_Uprising.

Chakravarty, Lalita, 'Emergence of an Industrial Labour Force in a Dual Economy — British India, 1880–1920', *The Indian Economic and Social History Review* (hereafter *IESHR*), vol. XV, no. 3, 1978, pp. 249–328.

Curtin, P.D., 'Sugar Prices and West Indian Prosperity', *The Journal of Economic History*, vol. XIV, no. 2, 1954, pp. 157–64.

Dasgupta, Ranjit, 'Factory Labour in Eastern India: Sources of Supply, 1855–1946', *IESHR*, vol. XIII, no. 3, July–September 1976, pp. 277–327.

Erickson, Edgar L., 'The Introduction of East Indian Coolies into the British West Indies', *The Journal of Modern History*, vol. VI, no. 2, June 1934, pp. 127–46.

Roberts, G.W. and J. Byrne, 'Summary Statistics on Indenture and Associated Migration affecting the West Indies, 1834–1918', *Population Studies*, vol. 20, no. 1, 1966, pp. 125–34.

Smith, Raymond T., 'Some Social Characteristics of Indian Immigrants to British Guiana', *Population Studies*, vol. 13, no. 1, 1959, pp. 34–9.

Unpublished Dissertations

Allen, Richard Blair, 'Creoles, Indian Immigrants and the Restructuring of Society and Economy in Mauritius, 1767–1885', unpublished Ph.D. dissertation, Michigan: University of Illinois, 1983.

Dhar, Sutapa, 'Changes in Occupational Structure and Economic Development of West Bengal, 1901–1991', Unpublished Ph.D. dissertation, Kolkata: Jadavpur University, 2001.

Ghosh, Chandralekha, 'Migration in West Bengal during the Period 1872–1991: An Empirical Analysis', Unpublished Ph.D. dissertation, Kolkata: Jadavpur University, 2001.

Index

Abolition Act of 1807 3
abolitionists 3
abuses or exploitation of immigrants 5,
     16, 62, 67
Act of Emancipation of 1834 77
Africans 3
Agra 35
agricultural labour, shortage of 4
Allahabad 37
Allen, Richard Blair 55
Anderson, C. 6
anti-indentureship campaign 79–80
anti-slavery movement 4
apprentice class 4
apprenticeship period 4
apprenticeship system, termination
     in 1838 14
Arrah 34, 55
Assam 33, 41
Azamgarh 34, 37, 55

Ballia 32, 44, 46
Basti 37
Bayley, Sir Stewart 32, 49
beet sugar, development of 14, 42
Bell, H. 69–70
Benares 34, 44–5, 55
Bengal 78, 80
   immigrants to the industrial districts
       of 45
   occupational structure of the working
       population in 46
   percentage of migrant workers in
       certain mills, factories and industrial
       concerns 44
   pressure of population in 49–50
Berbice 13
Bhagalpore 32, 34
Bihar 31–2, 34–5, 43, 46, 78
   economic hardship of people 32

British Guiana 4–5, 10, 35, 57, 59–60,
     78
   area 13
   economy and requirement for labour
       importation 13–16
   location 13
   religion and caste of emigrant,
       1865–1917 41
   sugar industry 13
   sugar legislation and impact on
       production 14
British Guiana Masters and Servants
     Ordinance, 1836 5
British land revenue policies in India 8
British mercantile houses 15
British plantation 3
   importation of slaves 3
British West Indies 4–5, 79
Browne, Lord H.U. 11
Burbank, Captain C. 49
Burdwan 34, 46

Calcutta Port 7, 16, 31, 35, 54, 65, 78
   emigrants from four sugar colonies
       proceeded to and returned for
       decades, 1842–1900 62, 82–5,
       96–101
   as zone of recruitment 8–10
Caribbean countries 3
caste and religion of emigrants 40–1
Central Provinces 46
Chattopadhyay, Haraprasad 77
cheap immigrant labourers 79
Chimmanlal 60
Chinese 62
Chotonagpur Plateau 9, 33, 46
Chuprah 34
cocoa 13
coffee 13
Colonial Authority for immigration 6

Comins, D.W.D. 42, 75
Committee of the British and Foreign
        Anti-Slavery Society 8
controlled emigration 5, 80
coolie emigration 5–8, 10
cost of emigration 62–7
Court of Directors of the East India
        Company 9
Creole agricultural labourer 58, 62–3
Crown colonies 3
Currie, Terrain 55

Darbhanga 32, 43
Darjeeling 43, 46
Demerara 7–8, 13, 35, 59, 61, 78
Dhangars 65
Dick, George R. 58
Dick, G.F. 6

Eales, Captain C. 69–70
education of the children of Indian
        immigrants 63
Elliott, T. 73
Emancipation Act of 1833 4
emancipation of slaves 14
emigrants, features of
    age 38–40, 86–9
    caste and religion 40–1, 92–5, 111
    corruption and organized crime among
        Indian immigrants 63
    drainage of wealth 79
    duties of the emigration agent 48
    life and condition of the Indian
        immigrants in 61, 66–7, 78
    place of origin 33–8
    remittances to India 76
    savings amounts of 58–9, 69
    sex ratio 40, 63, 90–1
    size of plots purchased by Indian
        immigrants, 1850–9 to 1880–4
        55–6
Emigration Act of 1871 78
emigration of Indian workers 109
    during 1872–3 33–4
    abolition of slave trade in 1834 31
    Annual General Administration
        Report of the Presidency Division
        for 1879–80 51
    annual number of labourers 6
    benefits from 17, 53–62
    from Bihar 31–2
    British Guiana 5
    changes in recruiting ground for 33–4
    contribution of Bengal 34
    coolies 5
    cost of 62–7
    economic factors and 78–9
    emigrants previously returned and
        re-emigrated 102–4
    emigrants previously returned from
        Mauritius and re-emigrated 102
    environmental factors 78–9
    famine-struck environment and 78–9
    fluctuation and its reasons 41–2
    ill-treatment and injustice against the
        Indians 61
    from India under the British rule 3
    Mauritius 4
    negative side of the planters' objectives
        and 79–80
    during period 1857–9 9
    protector of emigrants 16–17
    rules relating to 16
    terms of contract for 16–27
employment 4, 8, 32, 43, 51, 67
Essequibo 13
Evans, Revd Thomas 70

Farquhar, Sir Robert 3
Fergussan, W.F. 11
Fyzabad 37

Gangetic plains 78
Gaya 32–4, 43
Gazipur 55
Georgetown 13, 35
Ghazipur 34, 44, 46
Gladstone, John 4
Gladstone, William Ewart 4
Gonda 37
Gorakhpur 32, 37, 44–5
Gordon, Sir A. 71–2
Government of India Act XXI, 1844 5
Grant, J.G. 16, 42, 50, 72, 75
Grierson, George A. 7, 31, 33, 41, 59,
        61, 78

Harris, Lord 67
Hazaribagh 34
helpless and ignorant emigrants 64
Hesperus 5
Hill, Captain Thomas 11
hill coolies 33
history of emigration 3
Hobhouse, Sir Arthur 59
Hooghly 43, 46
Howrah 43–4

idlers and vagabonds 62
indebtedness 32, 79
indentureship 57, 59, 79–80
Indian diaspora 78
Indian emigrants, annual number of 6–7
Indo-Mauritians 53
Industrial Development in Bengal and
    inland labour demand 42–6
inland migration 42–6
    to tea districts of Assam 43
    towards Bengal 44–5

Jalpaiguri 43, 46
Jamaica 4–5, 8, 35, 63
    economy and requirement for labour
        importation 13–16
    emancipation of slaves in 1833 14
    sugar production 14
    termination of apprenticeship system
        in 1838 14
Jaunpur 37, 44
jute spinning and weaving 43–4

Kols 65
Kuczynski, Rene 7

landless labourers 8, 37, 80
Longden, Sir James 60
Lord Liverpool 3
loss of land rights 79
low-waged labour force 5
Lubbock, Nevil 59–60
Lucknow 37
Lushington, E.H. 11

macro-level effects on individual
    migrants 53

Madras 35, 46
Malagasy 3
malpractices by the recruiters 64
Mare, Belle 55
Mauritius 3–4, 61, 67, 78–9
    council of the government in 4
    district–wise distribution of emigrants,
        1851 and 1854–5 36
    economic life of 15
    immigration of Indian workers 4–6, 9
    life and condition of the Indian
        immigrants in 61
    location and area 15
    percentage of mortality in the vessel
        among the emigrants carried
        to 65–6
    plantation labour in 6
    proportion of immigrants from
        Bihar 34
    proportion of immigrants to 34
    purchase of land by Indian
        immigrants 34
    slaves 3
    sugar exports from 15
    sugar production in 15
    termination of 'apprenticeship'
        system 4
McNeill, James 57, 60
medical treatment for immigrants 60–1
micro-level effects on individual
    migrants 53
Midnapore 34
Monghyr 32, 34, 43
Monro, J. 51
Moravian missionary 63, 74
mortality among immigrants 65–6,
    106–8
Morton, Revd John 60
Muir, Sir William 70
Muir-Mackenzie, J.W.P. 54
Muzaffarpur 32, 34, 43

Nepal 46
North-Western Provinces (NWP) 31–2,
    34, 41–3, 78
    outmigrants of 46

Orissa 46

Oudh 34–5, 41–2, 78

Patna 32–4, 43
plantation industry 53
plantation labour in Mauritius 6
planters of West Indian colonies 4
Port Louis 9
poverty 79
Purulia 34

race discrimination 79
Ramdin, Rom 56
Ranchi 34
Raniganj coal mines 46
Real, Robert 5
recruiting labourers to colonies 3–5, 7
recruitment of efficient emigrants 80
Reddie, Captain John G. 68
Richard, V. 33
Rovertson, J.C. 64
Royal Commission in India, 1931 8
Royal Commission's report of 1872
    61

Salisbury, Lord 54–5
Sanderson Committee Report 57
Sarun 32, 43
Scoble, J. 8
sea journey 65
Secretary of State for the Colonies 3
sepoy recruitment 9
sex ratio of emigrants 40
Shahabad 9, 32–3, 37, 43
slave labour and protection 13
slave trade 3
Slave Trade Act in 1807 3
Smith, Raymond T. 34–41
steamships 65
sugar cane 13
sugar colonies 3, 7–8, 31, 34

economy and requirement for labour
    importation 13–16
fall in labour demand in 42
inducement to emigration terms and
    conditions 16–17
major 7–8
percentage of mortality in the vessel
    among the emigrants carried to
    65–6
price of sugar in European markets 15
push and pull factors for emigration 8
terms and contracts between the
    Government of India and 7
sugar industries 4
sugar production of colony 13–14

tax rolls 3
thefts and robberies 62
Trinidad 4, 8, 10, 35, 57, 59–61, 67
    area under cultivation 13
    economy and requirement for labour
        importation 13–16
    location 13
    a new island settlement 14
Truth and Justice Commission 67

unskilled labourers 78
UP 46
upsurge of nationalism 80

West Indian colonies 56
    mortality rate on the voyage 65
West Indian colonies, emigrants from
    Calcutta 9–10
West Indian planters 14
West Indian sugar industry 14
Whitby 5
working population in Bengal 46

Young, A.R. 68